Gretchen,
Never forget there's
a puppy in all of
us! Lesson 39.

Sandra Coyle

PS. I adore your
daughter! You raised
a purebred!!!

A tail wagging good time! Pure four-legged fun! One colossal treat! Hard to leave it! Two paws up!

Benji - New Yorkie Times

Bet you'll get caught with your wet nose in this book!

Gus - The Daily Beagle

Sanda Coyle has mastered tender dog tales and paired the lessons perfectly with people sense. Makes me want to come, sit, stay, and enjoy over and over and over.

Roxy - Bookwire Terrier

Meaty, full of delicious nuggets of wisdom. Lessons you can really sink your teeth into.

Stella - Pit Bull Post-Gazette

Great command of the English language! ***Surviving in a Dog Eat Dog World*** will make anyone learn why dogs are everyone's favorite people.

Sir Winston - Boston Terrier Globe

SURVIVING IN A DOG EAT DOG WORLD

A Instant Guide to Train People.

Sanda Coyle

SANDA COYLE

Illustrated by
MICHAEL COYLE

Fawn Cloud Press

This is for you Mom and Dad.

Foreword

It is a dog eat dog world out there. Everything seems faster. Everyone wants it now.

Buy me.

Take me.

Give me.

Show me.

Instant recognition.

Instant gratification.

Instant fame.

Instant fortune.

Instant coffee is no longer fast enough for most people. We need a Starbucks with a drive-thru on every corner. Meet you in an instant has given way to Instagram. Everyone wants it in a split second!

That is why you hold in your hand this little book. Yes, little —because it is so darn hard to find time to read these days. But just as important, I think of it as a *doggone* instant guide designed to train people with proven, practical life lessons. It's my mastery of simple principles learned over and over again (like a good trick) while working for some great (and not so great) companies. It's the product of being in some great and not-so-great relationships and raising some great but not always *perfectly* great kids for adulthood.

I have been owned by six dogs in my life, and I have been owned by two children. And for all intents and purposes, I have owned two husbands. On the career front, I have been owned by eight companies and have owned two companies.

Like each dog that found me, I found companies, careers, and people that (I believed) would provide me with happiness, rewards, a comfortable place to exercise my skills, and a forever-after. Like my dogs, I learned quickly. I served my masters well. I was loyal.

All that brought me here—to write *Surviving in a Dog Eat Dog World*. To respect privacy, many names have been changed. However, the stories and lessons learned are true. Now it's your turn to sit, stay, and learn a few new tricks.

Lesson 1:

Trust Your Instincts

Note to Self:
Dear Self,
I told you so.
Sincerely,
Your Instincts

Ever notice how a dog innately knows who to trust and who not to?

I have a friend who stops by the house. She comes across as a people person—kind, caring, giving. She is all smiles and full of gifts of words, deeds, and actual things. She lives her life in pursuit of likability.

That is why it is so strange that Sam, our 13-year-old Schnoodle, barks incessantly at her from the moment he sees her start to walk up the front steps. Sam stands seven inches above the ground and is around 15 pounds; however, when *this* friend comes by, he becomes a Great Dane.

I get it. Sam just doesn't like this friend. He backs away from her when she tries to give him a little scratch behind the ears. And he barks. My friend uses her sugary, sweet voice in a childlike tone, and Sam still barks. She ignores him, and he barks. She brings him treats—Sam's favorite thing in the world—and he barks. The harder she tries to acquire his affection, the more he lets her know that he is not about to change his perception of her. I think Sam is trying to tell us all something: I don't trust this person. I don't like this person. I am not going to let this person into my home.

Dogs know what they know. Their inner voice controls their outer voice. People have an inner voice as well. Sometimes they confuse it with a harsh, loud, overpowering dialogue inside their heads that reminds them of their foibles and failures. But that is *not* their inner voice. It's the voice of self-doubt and insecurity (more about that later). Your inner voice is that uh-oh feeling you get when you know someone (or something) just isn't right. It's the feeling you get when your true north is not facing north, when you are asked at work to bend more than you feel comfortable bending, when you feel like you just don't belong with the rest of the pack.

Listen carefully to that voice. Trust your instincts—just like Sam—because instincts are everything in business, in relationships, in partnerships, in friendships, in life. If you don't think you should do the deal, don't. If it sounds too good to be true, it is. If an employer promises you the moon during the interview stages of your relationship but won't put those promises in writing, they are most likely empty promises.

My husband, Robin, and I are volunteer mentors with a nonprofit career group in San Antonio, Texas. We help people find the right career. Most of the job seekers who come to our weekly support group have either been released to a new destiny because of downsizing, restructuring, relocation, or job elimination. Rarely are they looking for new jobs because of their great performance. In Texas, an at-will state (like so many other states), an employer can release an employee without cause. Most seekers come with a story of bitterness toward their former bosses, former companies, or former colleagues.

"My boss hated me from the day I started."

"I never fit in."

"No matter how hard I tried, they never gave me a chance to learn the systems. They wanted me to fail."

"No one ever talked to each other at work."

"They promised me time off and a flexible schedule and then told me I had to stay late."

Once these people peel back the layers, they discover that true north wasn't facing north. They had a feeling that the job just wasn't right for them. Most knew long before their elimination or release that their job just wasn't going well. Something was awry. They had an instinct that things were not good, but they ignored it. The voice was all but screaming inside their heads, but they didn't hear it. They didn't listen to it.

They needed some doggone good advice: **Trust your instincts!** Instead, they got up each morning, went through the mindless routine of getting ready for work, got dressed in suitable work attire, and headed out the door. Their stress level often increased as they passed each mile marker and got closer to their place of employment. At work, they found themselves in a no-win environment. They regularly doubted themselves and hated their work. Their attitude reflected in their productivity and relationships. At home, their miserable job situation made for an unhappy home life. The cycle of misery went on and on until either their job was eliminated or they were eliminated.

As I have worked with hundreds of these job seekers over the years, I've often wondered if they heard the voice *before* they took the job. Don't you wish there was an app you could download or a barcode you could scan before you took a job that would spit out your success/failure rate? Imagine that.

The same thing goes for employers who want to hire great

employees. Through the years, I have had the privilege of hiring hundreds of talented sales professionals, mid-level managers, and support staff. I have often been asked, "Is there an art or a science to hiring great people?" The short answer is yes. I have used questionnaires in the form of knock-out questions to screen candidates. I have used personality profiling from Myers-Briggs, StrengthsFinder, Enneagram, and Star Selection, all used by various corporate HR departments. Despite the data, what it always seemed to come down to was a gut feeling that told me the person was right (or wrong) for the job.

In a nutshell, companies don't hire people. People hire people. It is for that very reason that I share the story of the best hire I ever made: Scott.

I was the local sales manager for an NBC affiliate in San Antonio, Texas. Talent in our area was hard to find. The common statement was that the talent gene pool was shallow in San Antonio. I had been interviewing for media sales positions for quite some time.

One day, out of the clear blue, I was interrupted by a phone call from Scott. He had no sales experience. He had been a news photographer for the ABC affiliate I had worked for previously. I had no recollection of him, even though we had been at the same television station at the same time. I learned all that in a quick, maybe two-minute phone conversation. I asked him about his experience, and he openly said he had none. I ended the conversation abruptly. But there was something about that man that made him stand out in my mind. Keep in mind that this was before the days of social media and the instantaneous ability to profile people online.

Throughout the course of the next few weeks, Scott was relentless. He became a borderline professional stalker. He called. He wrote—very professional notes. He used every tactic he knew to get me to grant him an in-person interview, guaranteeing me it would not be a waste of my time. My practical nature told me to run away, fast, but my instincts told me otherwise.

I scheduled an interview with Scott. He arrived with a journal in hand and proceeded to show me firsthand how he would prospect clients and how he would use ideas and creativity to deliver results. He told me how his photography skills would be an asset to his creative process. Methodically and logically, he did everything he could to sell me on his abilities. Although his sales experience was zero, his sales skills were exceptional. It wasn't his tenacity that sold me; it was because he had *it*—that nameless quality that instinctively told me deep down inside that he was destined for greatness.

I hired Scott, and indeed, he did achieve everything I knew he would. He called on prospects and closed business deals that *no one* had ever been able to close. His clients were loyal, and they were profitable. As their businesses grew, Scott's revenue and income grew. He was my goose that laid the golden egg. During the years Scott worked for me, he proved his self-worth over and over again. My instincts had been spot-on. Scott will reign in history as the single best sales hire I have ever made. He has since moved on to bigger and better things, transforming into a close, personal, lifelong friend.

On the other end of the spectrum, when I was hired as a manager for the Meredith Television Station in Syracuse, New York, I inherited a salesperson on my team. Thomas was a young, dashing, handsome man of Italian descent. His dark hair, blue eyes, and olive skin made even the most proper woman look twice. He stood 5'10" with a muscular, chiseled frame. When I was introduced to him as his new manager, he greeted me in European fashion, taking my right hand into his, pulling me slightly forward and barely touching his cheek to mine as he delivered an "air kiss" to the side. I remember feeling that uh-oh feeling, but I could see precisely why he had been hired. He was a lady's man through and through. And his sales list consisted of accounts managed by young, single female agency buyers who all seemed to adore him.

Weeks into my tenure, I learned just how slick Thomas was. He signed out of the office for long periods of time without justification. He expensed lavish lunches with clients who never spent money with our station, and his paperwork had to be checked carefully for accuracy. Often, he added a few bonus commercials to someone's advertising schedule without justification or proper paperwork. Despite my boss's disagreement, I felt I needed to keep a close eye on Thomas.

One day, Thomas announced he was getting married to the daughter of one of New York's most prestigious personal injury attorneys. The attorney was a client of our station and one of our largest advertisers. His advertisements were those prolific ambulance chaser commercials that everyone hates. Thomas had been handling his now fiancé's father's account long before I was hired as his boss. But when an audit revealed that free bonus commercials had been added to most of the attorney's commercial schedules for months without justification, Thomas was moved off of the account. I argued that this indiscretion was grounds for termination, but my boss demanded that Thomas remain on the team. After all, I had only been his manager for a few weeks, and I needed to give him a chance to prove himself to me.

I continued to have that gut feeling that, with Thomas, there was much more I needed to be worried about. Two weeks later, I was at home watching CBS. It was Sunday night, and *60 Minutes* was just starting. Before the show began, a local jeweler's commercial came on. The jeweler had become a personal friend of mine, and I knew his business and advertising budget well. I immediately thought, there is no way *that* jeweler could afford a 30-second commercial on *60 Minutes*! He doesn't spend that much money on advertising in a month!

Monday morning, I came into the station and checked orders, invoices, and affidavits. There were thousands of dollars in free, no-charge commercials that had been aired for the jeweler. All the paperwork just didn't add up. I picked up the phone and called the jeweler. "Brad," I said. "I am here trying to get my arms around paperwork, and I am looking at about $10,000 in no-charge, free commercials we have aired for you. Can you help me understand why?" Brad answered without hesitation. Thomas had come to him and offered a commercial airtime advertising schedule in exchange for a $12,000 diamond engagement ring. My instincts were right. Thomas was subsequently fired.

When you hear that voice or have that gut feeling, trust your instincts.

I am fairly certain that animals, especially dogs, do not have voices in their heads reminding them of their failures or foibles. Clearly, I'm sure that some of my dogs have never heard those voices. Had they, I am sure Sam, our Schnoodle, would have never tried to sneak a Hershey's kiss again. The reminder of the outcome and subsequent vet visit would surely keep him from begging for kisses—which he continues to do. But we are not dogs; we are humans and occasionally hear faint voices in our heads. Sometimes, those instinctive voices remind me of important things like how significant I am and that I am truly blessed by friends, family, and co-workers. Other times, my voices tell me that I might fail, that I am not good enough, that I don't measure up to others, that I am not worthy. Those voices are *not* voices of instinct; they are voices of self-doubt and insecurity. The quickest way to lose, the quickest way to fail, the quickest way to quit is to buy into those voices.

Over the years, when those self-doubting voices rear their ugly heads, I channel my inner dog. When the voice of doubt shrieks failure, I think of Sam lusting after another Hershey's kiss. When the voice of doubt tells me I am not worthy, I hear the word *treat*. When the voice of doubt says "I can't," I hear the words *let's go!* and get as excited as Sam does for the next adventure. I agree with my Sam—I never hear the word *no* unless it's my instincts talking.

As for my friend at the front door who Sam barks at, my instincts tell me that she is a good person. My experience and knowledge prove that it's true, and so, despite Sam's irritating voice of disapproval, she remains my dear friend. As for Sam, his instincts turned out to be spot on. My friend is a cat person. Sam will no doubt continue to bark at her when she arrives at the front door. She will attempt to charm him, but deep down, I know Sam knows there is the smell of cat on her hands—the hands that are trying to pet him.

Lesson 2:

Leave Your Mark

Own who you are, what you believe in, and what you have done.

O ur first Schnoodle was Fay, a gift to our son Michael for his ninth birthday. He wanted a ferret, but the adults in the house outvoted him, and he got a dog instead. Fay was a Continental Club papered purebred (miniature Poodle and miniature Schnauzer). She had poodle legs and a sleek, pint-sized, greyhound-like grey body. She was a walker and a jumper. Walks, which were her favorite pastime, usually took up to an hour in order to somewhat tire her out. She would sprint and then stop abruptly to leave her mark. I always wondered if she believed the entire neighborhood was hers. She sometimes marked her territory 20 times during her sojourn. In her Schnoodle mind, it was her yard, her fence, her mailbox, her hydrant, and her stop sign. I am sure every pet in the neighborhood understood that Fay (all 9½ pounds of her) was in charge.

Over the years, I have learned that leaving your mark is

as important as doing a great job. Often, it is more important. I learned that the hard way. I have never been good at letting my companies know that the idea, the concept, the sell, the great hire, the proposal, and the win were mine. I rarely took credit. Instead, I was always quick to hold up the team or individual sales account manager with accolades. Somewhere in my leadership development and training, I forgot the vowel *I* and, instead, let everyone else receive the praise and attention. After all, wasn't that what servant leadership was all about? The answer is a resounding no! In today's dog eat dog world, leaving your mark and letting everyone know that you own it, you did it, and you are responsible for it is truly key.

When I was a local sales manager at an ABC affiliate in Texas, I became branded as the "idea person" who could wow anyone with a great idea. Over the course of five years, the sales team and higher management came to me for the next iteration of themed sales opportunities they could create and sell. Need a concept for a hospital? Go to Sanda. Need an idea for an automotive dealership to move used cars? Sanda will create it and go with you on the call to make sure the client loves it. Need a way to sell the NBA Finals? Sanda will stay late, create the presentation, and host the client event to present it.

At that stage of my life, I had been managing people for more than 20 years. So you think I would have known better. But here's when my eyes were opened. Corporate raised sales commissions for new business as an incentive to grow sales revenue, and my sales account executives' incomes rose sharply —because of my great ideas and sales efforts. Don't get me wrong, growing my team and the station's revenue was my job as a manager. But the job lost its glamour when my individual efforts directly pole-vaulted others' income into the higher tax brackets and I remained a mid-level manager in title and compensation. As their sales incomes rose sharply, corporate wanted to know why our station was doing so well.

So corporate installed big brother—real-time monitors—on the walls of the sales office in an effort to track individual revenue versus individual activity. Then they shared the data with our sister stations and the corporate C-suite. Suddenly, my salespeople were not only increasing their commissions by tens of thousands of dollars monthly, but corporate was holding them up *individually* for what appeared to be their magnificent efforts and great ideas.

Again, my Puritan ethics and servant leadership kicked in, and I continued to support my people and help them look good because I wanted to be a great manager. It wasn't until corporate froze managers' salaries in a cost-cutting effort that it became perfectly clear to me that my position could easily become expendable in the eyes of higher management and corporate. After all, there was no indication that I had contributed to my sales team's success. They were getting all the glory and making all the money.

I have often wondered how much it cost me over the years to *not* leave my mark. Had I been overlooked for other career opportunities because others felt I had not proven I had the skills? Did others simply not know what I did? I read an article recently that said that women give luck more credit for their success than themselves. Clearly, in the past, I had been lucky to surround myself with good people. I have worked for good companies with good leadership at the helm. But when bad people, bad leadership, and not-so-good companies make decisions based on the information they are provided, isn't it wise to make sure you've left your mark? Don't you deserve the credit? After all, if no one knows what is yours, how will you ever be able to take ownership?

I have always had first-grade-teacher handwriting, each letter perfectly formed. Since my early years, my printing has looked almost like I used stencils. In third grade, I was in class with David. Today, David would be considered a bully, but back then, he was just considered mischievous. School was easy for me. I learned quickly and enjoyed everything about school. Along with my perfect handwriting was my need to be top in my class.

So the day Mrs. Kramer, my third-grade teacher, asked me why I hadn't turned in my assignment, I was petrified. Surely she must have lost it. I remember crying and telling her I had turned in my paper. She insisted it was not there and told me I would have to redo the work after school. After school? Even at age eight, I am fairly certain I knew I wasn't one of those kids that had to stay after school! Maybe it was the tears. Maybe it was my pathetic look as I stood before Mrs. Kramer with my pouty lips quivering, but Mrs. Kramer decided to take one last look at the stack of collected assignments.

There, about halfway through the pile of 28 papers, was David's paper, or at least what appeared to be David's paper, for David's name was written at the top. On closer review, it became apparent that David had taken my paper, tried to erase my name at the top, smeared it, and then tried to cover up the smear. He had partially crossed out my name and finally added his own name. David's name was at the top of the paper. I am sure it must have looked odd—David's serial-killer handwriting at the top of what was a perfectly penned, stencil-perfect paper.

In an attempt to take credit for something not his, David had left his mark. David was sent to the principal's office for cheating, and I must have been redeemed since I didn't have to stay after school. Even as a third grader, the experience of leaving your mark had been etched into me.

D ogs mark everything, right? I loved watching Schnoodle Fay circle around on a blanket, almost wearing out the pile until she made the blanket hers and finally settled in for the night. Fay knew her pillow, her bed, her blanket, her toys. They had her magical scent on them. When she came home from the groomer, she ran around the house like a crazy dog, rubbing against everything as if she needed to remark every item with her new, freshly shampooed scent. Once that ritual was complete, she made a beeline to the backyard so she could roll around on her back and wipe off the pungent, sweet smell of fresh dog shampoo. Then she came back in the house and repeated the rubbing routine.

Fay's toys were definitely her toys. She loved them best when they became gnarly, pilly, and wet after she sucked on them, leaving her mark. Fay had toys that were her favorites, and she never confused them with our other dog's toys. Fay owned them. They were hers; she had marked them. She also left her mark on our lives for more than 14 years. Fay lived to be almost 100 in dog years, leaving our home in September 2016. Her greatest mark was the one she left on our family's hearts.

I became the de facto intellectual property police at iHeart Media back when it was publicly traded under the name Clear Channel Radio. I wasn't hired to protect the company's copyrighted trademarks, but it became my responsibility under the "other duties as necessary" heading. Basically, I was the keeper of the Clear Channel Radio logo, name, and all the 1,600 logos and names of our 1,600 radio stations throughout the United States. I controlled the trademark and made sure others did not use it in any form or variation unless they had permission.

Occasionally, someone would try to capitalize on our brand name and use our logo for promotional purposes. After all, being associated with the world's largest radio company had its benefits. But the biggest culprits were our very own employees and stations that always tried to use the copyright or trademark on everything without permission. Often, local stations would alter the protected logo, change the colors, revamp it, or add objects to it so it would fit their station's seasonal or promotional needs. You can imagine how frustrating it was to see the logo of the number-one radio station in New York with a red and white Santa's hat pasted on top of it. Cleaning up the infractions was almost a full-time job. Employees seemed to feel that since they worked for Clear Channel, they owned everything associated with Clear Channel and could use protected intellectual property and trademarks as they saw fit.

Occasionally, the problem was not using our protected mark. I reported to John, the CEO of radio as his senior vice president. John was a great leader and even better operations man. He was fair, honest, and overly generous. More often than not, he showered his top managers with gifts and accolades. He made way for top managers to get the best of training and best-in-class resources. Then he made sure they were touted for their personal greatness in their individual markets. Careers of his top leaders soared as they became known for their innovation and expertise, much of which was orchestrated, designed, and created by John himself.

John was also compelled to support many causes. He bought tens of thousands of dollars of tables at fundraising events. He donated hundreds of thousands of items and airtime to charities. He was an extraordinarily cheerful giver, but he never wanted his name on anything. Clear Channel as a company didn't get any public credit for the vast donations, and John never wanted anyone to know he had personally arranged the giving.

As Clear Channel went private and ultimately became iHeart Media, the press had a field day. Headlines implied that Clear Channel was a stingy company that never took care of its people or the communities it served. In the end, Clear Channel, with John at the helm, was plagued with destroying local radio and homogenizing the industry. On the day of its privatization, the stock was at a low point, and many of the key executives, leaders, and best employees who were given stock options as incentives for great work were upside down in their options and walked away with nothing.

I often wondered how things would have been different had John gotten credit for all the great things he had done. What if John's great actions had been more known, more visible to others? What if John had chosen to leave his mark? What would the press headlines have been then?

I left Clear Channel in 2009. I left genuinely believing that Clear Channel Radio was not responsible for the death of local radio. Radio changed in the 2000s. Technology evolved, and the way people got their information and music changed. Ironically, Clear Channel was at the forefront of most of the innovation. But nobody (including John) got credit for it.

Dogs get credit for everything they do. They leave their mark and claim ownership of their territory. We, too, need to leave our mark—we need to take credit for our work (both good and bad). We need to imprint our work product with our proverbial signature. We need to let the world know we own it!

Lesson 3:

Have Lots of Toys

Play. Have fun. Learn how to make money. Having fun and making money bring both joy to the bottom of your heart and joy to the bottom line.

There is a large, hand-woven African basket in our house. It is a good 3 feet in diameter and stands 15 inches off the ground. It tilts to one side, partly because it has never regained its perfect shape since its packaging and shipping days and partly because its lopsided shape allows easy side access for our Schnoodle Sam. It sits next to the chest at the end of our bed. It was given to me by my sister Crystal. Everyone in my family has one. Most of them have tightly placed, rolled-up couch blankets in their baskets. Mine holds toys—Sam's toys. It is the place of honor where all toys—new and used, mangled, fresh out-of-the-package-perfect, squeakerless, and squeakers intact—live. Dog toys are part of our house and frequently pepper the floor that was once covered with stray Legos and assorted *Goosebumps* paperbacks. Sam is our fur-child. He has been coined our "play, dog, play" baby.

Sit in a chair in the living room, ignore Sam, and watch what happens. One by one by one, Sam will bring you a toy. First, it's Bear, a small, 3-inch brown bear that wears overalls, has ropes for legs, and sports a slightly chewed-off nose. Sam will drop him at your feet, back away a few inches, and then growl at you as if to say, "Pick it up. Throw it." Ignore Sam, and he will growl again. After three to five attention-getting growl attempts with no reaction, Sam will strut back into the bedroom and retrieve another toy from the African basket. He returns to the living room and this time drops at your feet a red-and-black slipper with the word *Fashionista* embroidered on it. Sam, seeing no reaction from you, will begin to pick up the slipper, toss it into the air, and let it fall at your feet again. This action is followed by another growl. Still no human reaction? Sam sprints into the bedroom and returns with Green Stuffed Broccoli that crinkles like tissue paper when he maneuvers it around in his mouth. Reactionless human? Sam continues his methodical retrieve-growl-toss-growl game until on the floor in front of you are the Weiner Dog, Big Dino, Pink Bunny (with one ear missing), Santa (with half a mustache chewed off), Baby Blue Dino, Baked Potato, little Lamb Chop that lost its sound, Big Lamb Chop that is bald on the front cheek, and Red Lobster with one eye chewed off and no filling in either claw. Sam has honed his play-with-me process to the point that even the most die-hard, anti-dog visitors will reluctantly pick up a toy and throw it for him. Sam loves his toys.

To many visitors, I am sure that Sam's game, coupled with the abundance of toys, is overwhelming. No dog, they must be thinking, should ever have that many toys. Surely, in their eyes, he is spoiled. However, I have come to realize that having lots of toys is a very good thing both for Sam and for me.

W hen I was hired as Senior Vice President of Strategic Marketing for Clear Channel Radio, the responsibility came with a corner office on the second floor of Clear Channel Communications' corporate offices in San Antonio, Texas. The layout of the second floor resembled a square donut. One side overlooked the green fairways of a private golf course. The other sides, including my window, faced a very robust shopping mall and strip center. In the middle of the second-floor offices were cubicles for support staff. Much to my surprise, my office was directly catty-corner to all of the C-suite executives on the floor. That included the executive suites for the family members who started Clear Channel—Lowry Mays, Mark Mays, and Randall Mays. The offices were elegantly decorated with expensive wood paneling and cabinetry, along with lighted, built-in cases that displayed a collection of vintage radios. On the walls were sizable and impressive art collections, including (my personal favorite) a Lichtenstein.

Settling into a new space takes time and usually involves a special day on a weekend to carry in all your personal belongings. On move-in day at Clear Channel, I rearranged the furniture and pushed a large bookcase up against the wall to the left of the door. Its new location now made it visible to passersby. Next, I relocated my desk and credenza near the street-facing windows so I could watch the mall shoppers. I put the guest chairs near the side of the desk so I could create a conversation and teamwork atmosphere. Finally, I began to unpack my boxes.

First out of the boxes were electronic singing and dancing animated dolls. Each stood $2\frac{1}{2}$ feet tall. There was Bing Crosby holding a floor microphone and donning a red and white felt Santa's hat. When you pushed his button, he swayed back and forth and sang "White Christmas." Next was Dean

Martin in his black tux and pressed white shirt. When activated, he sang "That's Amore" and "Everybody Loves Somebody Sometime." Then there was Louis Armstrong singing "Hello Dolly" followed by "What a Wonderful World." The fourth and final figurine was James Brown dressed in leather pants and a leather vest, crooning "I Feel Good" while his hips swayed to the beat. All were placed proudly on the large bookcase in easy sight of any passerby.

Next was a basket of juggling balls, a Magic 8 ball, a collection of magic wands from the original Magic Kingdom, and every foam stress squeeze shape ever imagined. The basket seemed perfect and easily accessible on the corner of my desk. Finally, packed carefully in clear Ziploc bags, were about 100 wind-up toys I had collected from all over the world in the past 20 years or so. To me, the perfect spot to display them for everyone to enjoy was on the windowsills inside the French panes of glass that faced the common walkway on the second floor. I carefully placed each small wind-up toy by groups. There was the Disney collection, the Simpsons collection, and the entire collection of Smurfs, all purchased in the early 1980s. Next were the religious wind-ups, including the walking nun, Moses, David, and Noah. The last to be placed on the windowsills were the random animals, fairies, walking toasters, clacking teeth, the TV, and assorted cars.

My toy collection started in 1987 when I first became a manager. To me, toys placed strategically around an office exemplified fun and softened the heart of almost any stressed-out salesperson, hard-nosed client, or small child waiting for mom or dad to finish up a project. I simply loved them and wanted to see people engaged in play as they solved the problems of the entertainment world.

My father collected toys. He loved toy tractors and farm machinery of all kinds. He often said that his immense collection was making up for all the toys he didn't have as a child growing up in rural Ohio during the Depression. His massive collection required a special room adjacent to my parents' home. My mom said they had to stay out there, out of sight, so she wouldn't have to dust them. (I always found that ironic because my mom never dusted anything!) So, Dad built shelves and found cases for each of his best tractors. The rest were organized by size and year and stored in cases in their original boxes.

With my office perfectly oozing pure Sanda toy joy, I picked up the empty containers and shut my office door behind me. I would return bright and early on Monday morning. The start of a new job and a new work week always enthralled me. When Monday arrived, I all but raced into the building and headed excitedly toward the second floor with my office keys in hand.

As I rounded the corner, I almost knocked down a small, older woman who had parked what appeared to be her 5-foot frame smack dab in front of the French pane window wall of wind-ups. Her short, streaked grayish-blond hair was tousled, almost disheveled, and her well adorned rhinestone-blinged long-sleeved top came down over her elastic-waist velour pants. On her feet were a cross between slippers and house shoes. They too, were adorned with rhinestone bling. At first glance, I thought she was part of our support staff or cleaning crew.

As I fumbled to regain my balance and apologize profusely for all but immobilizing her, she looked up at me and said, "Whose office is this?" I remember hesitating at first, but the keys in my hands soon gave away the answer that the office was mine. I quickly inserted the key, turned the knob, and unlocked the door. It was then that I revealed the rest of the toys and figurines. "Hi, I'm Sanda Coyle," I said and tried to meet her hand in a civil and professional exchange. She pushed her small frame into the office and began to take in all the color and frivolity. I followed behind her.

"We have strict office decor policies here at Clear Channel," she insisted. "Everyone is required to get approval before they (she motioned toward the toys) decorate. Aren't you the new marketing person?" she asked. I nodded my head yes. "Then, I guess this (she motioned again at the toys) will work. Besides," she added, "your office is back in the corner away from other executives."

I later found out that the woman was Mrs. Peggy Mays, wife of Lowry Mays, the largest shareholder and chairman of Clear Channel Communication, our parent company. As it turned out, I would be one of the few people ever allowed to deviate from the office decorum.

There is a thick line between playing *at* work and playing *for* work. Playing *at* work often meant you were goofing off. It was the act of being paid for your time by the company as you slacked off, horsed around, or just failed to be productive. But for me, playing *for* work has always been a creative ritual. It is the art of using colorful, fun, creative objects to get the wheels in my head turning. The end product of playing for work is always a great idea, an innovation, or a problem solved. Having toys in my office promotes playing for work. So it came to be that toys have been in every office I have ever had, and playful fun time has always been encouraged.

In order to be successful in business, I believe you have to both have fun and make money. To only make money without having fun usually resulted in not wanting to keep my job. To have fun without making money for the company for which I worked could have also easily resulted in not keeping my job. Having fun and making money both bring joy to the bottom of my heart and joy to the bottom line. So play. Have fun.

Lesson 4:

Be The First To Wake Up

Time is money.

Early to bed, early to rise, makes a man healthy, wealthy, and wise.

Lost time is never found again.

—Benjamin Franklin

There are two types of people: morning people and non-morning people. There is only one type of dog.

I am a morning person. My favorite part of the day is when the sun is barely peeking out of the sky, when the street-lights are still on and the yard is illuminated by the front porch light. I love the smell of a new day followed by the smell of a freshly brewed cup of coffee. I have never owned a dog that didn't enjoy getting up early with me. Maybe it was the sound of the birds, the weekly garbage trucks, the alarm going off, or the anticipation that their food bowl would be filled. But all of my fur children have always enjoyed getting up early.

Morning was our time together. Most days now involve

walks around the neighborhood just as the sun is rising, but for years, my morning routine always resulted in the greatest productivity. It was drilled into my head that the early bird catches the worm. And the rooster-crow start of the day never had to be learned by Greta.

Greta was a rescue who happened into my life long before I had children. I was living in Central New York when my first husband, Ed, came home from work one fall night with a year-old German Shepherd. Ed was a news anchor in the adjacent city of Utica, New York. He worked for a very wealthy family-owned company that had invented Duncan Hines boxed cake mixes and decided to invest their cake mix wealth in television stations. The staff at the TV station was minimal at best. The station existed on a shoestring budget, but it was a great place to begin a career in broadcasting.

Ed commuted daily from our home in Cazenovia, New York, on the New York State Thruway to Utica. He anchored both the 6:00 p.m. and 11:00 p.m. newscasts. His commute took him away from home around 2:00 p.m. every day, and he returned around 2:00 a.m. the following morning. While coming down the hill heading away from the Utica TV station, one of Ed's co-workers spotted a stray. Greta was small for her breed and very thin. She was skittish and hated to be around children or bicycles. After trying temporary homes in the apartments of Ed's co-workers, Ed decided he needed to bring Greta to our large home and large yard in Cazenovia.

I had been around German Shepherds all my life since they were one of my father's favorites. Often, my dad would get a call from a former law officer friend, and he would become the new owner of a retired German Shepherd police dog. The dogs were extremely intelligent and loyal, and they made great watch dogs for my dad's auction lots. Greta eventually looked as majestic as any of the retired police dogs, but she was shy and yearned for a forever family.

At first, Greta stayed close by my side and avoided roaming the house. It wasn't until she was outside that she would run like the wind. Her running created a rather small but expensive problem. Our yard was a little over an acre of beautiful, well-manicured lawn and landscaping, but there was no fence in which to contain our new skittish, running dog. The small second-story deck on the back of our split-level house was perfect for her to lie in the sun and look out high over the yard. It was perfect until Greta spotted a deer and jumped from her second-story perch onto the yard below to chase it. We decided that Greta would become an inside dog until we could save money and partially fence the yard.

Greta learned our schedules quickly.

The man leaves hours after lunchtime in the afternoon when the sun is bright in the sky. He takes the small car and comes home when the stars are out and the lady is asleep. The lady gets up before the sun comes up, only a few hours after the man returns home, and goes first to the kitchen and gets something in a cup that smells better than it tastes. Then she goes into the square, small room (next to the round, eye-level water bowl that always has cold water in it), takes off her clothes, and gets wet. The man sleeps soundly while the lady is getting wet.

The lady comes out of the wet box and carefully rummages through the small dark room filled with clothes, picks many items, and adds layers of them over the top of each other until she is completely covered. She then goes back into the room with the wet box and round, eye-level water bowl (that I love), gets out the wind-blowing wand, and blows the fur on her head. Sometimes she also blows me in the face. It is warm, and I like that.

Then she uses small brushes that aren't very tasty and puts stuff on her face. (It, too, is not tasty.) Once she is covered and fluffy and has stuff on her face, she heads toward the kitchen, and that is when I get fed. After food, the lady leaves me and goes away in the big car, and I watch the man sleep until he gets up and goes into the wet box room.

Greta greeted me at the mud room door every evening when I returned from work around 6:15. She followed me into the kitchen and waited patiently for me to fix both of our dinners. Once dinner was done, nighttime activities completed, Greta settled into her favorite spot beside the bed on the floor next to whichever human she was responsible for at the time. From 9:00 p.m. until 5:30 a.m., it was me. From 2:00 a.m. to 12:00 noon, it was Ed.

At night, I often worried that if I were to get up suddenly, I might step on Greta as she slept on the floor next to my side of the bed. One night, after too many cups of hot tea to warm me through the blustery Central New York winter night, I awoke and needed to go to the bathroom. It was then that I discovered Greta was already awake and alert before my feet hit the carpet. Poised to assist in any way possible, she had instinctively learned to be the first one to wake up.

I tested the theory again and again. Alarm goes off at 5:30 a.m., covers jostle to untangle feet from the bottom of the bed, leg slips out, Greta is standing, waiting. Same thing happened to Ed. Alarm goes off at 12:00 noon, Greta is there staring at him, alert and waiting.

Years went by. Greta got her fenced-in yard, and we had our first child, Kimberly, who was also our parents' first grandchild. We took careful steps to make sure Kimmy was safe. At the coaxing of her grandfather, we removed the door to her bedroom and replaced it with a wooden screen door so we could easily see and hear her, but Greta wouldn't be able to get in the room. As the first weeks went by and somewhat of a routine was established, Greta chose to park herself in front of Kimmy's door all night and during the day whenever she was sleeping. At the first sound of Kimmy moving, Greta would rise, stretch, and head to Ed or me as if to alert us that Kimmy needed our attention. As Kimmy got older, the screen door was left open more and more, and Greta found her spot next to the crib where Kimmy slept. Greta was always the first to wake, greet Kimmy, and then come and find us.

Greta was not my only dog that woke up first in the morning. In fact, all my dogs have woken up before I did. Maybe it is simply so they don't get accidentally stepped on or tousled out of the bed by my movements. However, I think there is a bigger reason—a more purposeful reason that dogs wake up early. It is so they can be ready, alert, and the first to respond. And those reasons are sound—sound enough that anyone should base their professional and personal lives on them.

As a mother, I have found that being ready, alert, and the first to respond was a big plus for my children, my children's friends, their parents, and their teachers. Being the first to wake up meant we were always on time, prepared, and ready to take on any Mom-oh-by-the-way-I-need moments!

I n business, being ready, alert, and first to respond got me many job promotions, new accounts, or just a win. People respect timeliness, eagerness, and those who are first. Many a deal has been done at an early breakfast meeting. And what about your personal appointments? Don't want to wait in line at the Department of Motor Vehicles, at a doctor's office, at an attorney's office, at a meeting with your accountant? Be the first appointment of the day. It works every time.

I am not a big sports fanatic, but I *was* trained to believe that if you practice right, you play right. That lesson was instilled in me by a tough sales manager at a radio station group in Central New York. His name was Chuck, and prior to becoming a sales manager, he must have been a high school football coach. Chuck's theory was that if you gave your all on the field during practice (in essence, practice right), then when it was game time and it mattered most, you would play to win (thus play right). Practicing right meant being early for his sales meetings and prepared with notebook and pen, ready to take notes. You were also expected to have a comprehensive understanding of where your book of business was at any given time and be ready to go on a sales call at any moment with sales materials, current rate cards, inventory sheets, and sales packages printed and ready to go. Chuck's "practice right" also included having no less than a half a tank of gas in your car at any time so you would not have to stop for gas before you went on an appointment.

To Chuck, punctuality was vital. "If you arrive late for me," he shouted, "you will arrive late for a client. Late ain't great!" During my short stint under his leadership, our offices were downtown. Parking, if you could find it, was often blocks away. Sales meetings started precisely at 8:00 a.m. At 8:01 a.m., Chuck literally locked the doors and would not allow you to come in. On those mornings, my commute time was an hour, and then I spent 15 minutes circling the block in my car to find parking. And then there was the 15-minute sprint in heels and eventually in stocking feet to get to the office. If the elevator didn't arrive right away, I added five flights of stairs to my commute before I turned the handle to the sales conference room door and stood there panting like some overworked dog.

Once—and only once—was the door locked when I arrived. The humiliation burned in my face, and the nightmare of the experience still floods my mind with angst. I can only imagine what my peers sitting around the conference room table must have thought as I struggled frantically to manipulate the door handle so it would somehow open the locked door. And of course, they could see all the commotion through the floor-to-ceiling glass. That was the day I learned to practice right, be the first to wake up, and definitely be the first to arrive.

Over my decades as a manager, I would say that most employee reprimands have been from inconsistent adherence to office hours. Simply getting employees to show up to work on time created all kinds of HR nightmares. Somewhere in the consensus, group-think office concept, it has become socially acceptable for employees to meander into work on their own—not the company's—schedule. The days of locking the door have long passed, but the idea of punctuality still deserves respect. Imagine how much more productive today's work force would be if employees simply arrived on time.

I believe great leadership begins with self-discipline. Be like Greta—be the first to wake up! And remember what Ben Franklin said: "Time is money. Early to bed, early to rise, makes a man healthy, wealthy, and wise. Lost time is never found again."

Always Make an Entrance

Do you want to make a difference in the world?

It starts with how you enter a room.

Always make an entrance. Not a *look-at-me* or a *here-I-am* entrance, but with genuine confidence that lets everyone know you are really glad to be there.

On Sunday nights, a group of 16 to 20 people meets in our home for a potluck dinner and a Bible study discussion group. The group has now become our San Antonio family. We are so familiar with each other that people no longer ring the doorbell. They let themselves in, put their covered dish on the counter, and help themselves to something to drink. Sam (you remember our dog Sam) has come to expect guests on Sunday nights. Somewhere in his little Schnoodle brain, I really believe he thinks everyone is coming to see *him*.

Once the last person arrives, Sam makes his way through the kitchen, living room, and dining room to personally greet everyone. First, he rubs up against a few legs. That results in the traditional pat on the head followed by the scratch behind the ears. Next, he seeks out those who respond more to verbal praise. Planting himself in front of them (almost blocking their ability to move), Sam gives a low, guttural growl. The human response is always "Hi, Sam." Finally, he seeks out those who gravitate toward the couch (*his* couch) and pushes on his back loins in an attempt to jump up and join them. Usually, Sam tries three or four times before he actually leverages enough torque to push himself up and over the ottoman and onto the couch. Once there, he plunders for the nearest couch toy and drops it onto someone's lap. Playtime ensues. And then there are the latecomers. Sam greets them with an I'm-in-charge-but-welcome-to-my-home-anyway bark. That group, we have come to find out, is not-particularly-fond-of-dogs people.

I have watched Sam every Sunday night for months as he refines his greeting. The leg-rub people are never couch-jump people. His guttural-growl friends are very different from the don't-like-dogs-so-I-must-bark-at-them people. Sam instinctively knows. He knows these people and greets them perfectly, matching who they are with a precise response.

No one made a better entrance than Duke did. Duke was a full-sized German Shepherd. He was a police dog retired from the Chicago Police Department. His broad chest pushed out almost as if he were in military stance at all times. His ears were always perfectly pointed and alert. He was regal, beautiful, and very confident. Duke was a gift to my father, and he immediately became his favorite dog. Duke served both my father and my mother as a beloved companion and an exceptional guard dog.

My parents owned an auction business that sold heavy equipment, surplus, and retired vehicles for all the major utility companies in the Southwest. Auction day was busy, almost frantic, with hundreds of bidders all vying for the highest bid on choice and often hard-to-find used machinery. Everyone in my family worked the sales, but my mother seemed to have the most tedious job. She was in charge of settling all the purchases and collecting the money. Cash, cashier's checks, or certified funds were the only forms of payment. As a result, literally hundreds of thousands of dollars in cash exchanged hands in a single workday.

On auction day, prior to the sale, Dad would take Duke on a leash past the crowd and head straight into the business office where my mother handled the money. Duke held his head high, legs almost marching in procession. Dad held the leash taut, pulling slightly, which made Duke push his chest out even further. Everyone noticed. No one dared distract Duke from his parade. Once inside the office, Dad unleashed Duke, who then positioned himself at my mom's side, right behind her desk. He went down on his haunches, paws straight forward, ears up, and eyes alert until after the auction was over.

Throughout the day, successful bidders formed a line in front of the office door and one by one entered and settled their purchases. As hundred-dollar bills were counted and vehicle titles filled out, Duke sat calmly, but with purpose. You could not be in the office without feeling Duke's presence or seeing his massive shape next to his master. He almost begged for a command to take down anyone who dared cross my mom.

Every dog makes an entrance. Some walk in playfully; others have an air of tenacity, and others walk with their tail between their legs in dishonor. People make entrances, too. I have interviewed literally hundreds of people for various positions, and I can assure you, I always noticed how they came into the building and then into my office. Was I impressed by those who entered like Duke—with purpose, with a commanding stance, with head held high? The answer is a resounding *yes*! On the other hand, those who could barely get their name out, had their eyes down and shoulders pulled in all but shouted "Unconfident!"

When I first met my husband Robin on a blind date (my first and only blind date), he arrived very late due to a weather delay. He had driven from Fort Worth to San Antonio to meet me for dinner. In normal conditions, the drive is four and a half hours, but with torrential rainstorms, his trip took him close to six and a half hours. That meant I waited close to two hours at the restaurant, and of course, I was too proud to leave and admit I had been stood up.

When Robin entered the restaurant, he had a crooked grin on his face. His overcoat was wet, drenched with rain, and his feet were tracking in water. His hair was wet, and soaked strands streaked down his forehead. He looked like he had just been through war, hell, or both, but he was still smiling. He greeted me with a large, overpowering (wet) hug and a voice that was equally big and loud.

Anyone who knows me knows that I am a stickler for punctuality. But this rain-soaked, middle-aged man had entered this crowded restaurant and was literally standing in his man-made puddles of confidence—and that overshadowed his tardiness. How could anyone fault him for being late? He had just spent six and a half hours behind the wheel of a motor vehicle, driving in the rain to meet me for the first time.

Don't get me wrong. Being late is not an acceptable practice in most life scenarios, but it was Robin's confidence and self-assuredness that made this time-keeping, watcher-of-watches give him a chance.

I was interviewing candidates once for a marketing position

at an NBC station. I had scheduled a 2:00 p.m. interview with Carmen. On paper, Carmen was a seasoned professional with more than 10 years of marketing experience. She also had an extensive creative and graphics background, which I felt could fill multiple roles for one salary. As 2:15 p.m. rolled around, I called down to the front desk receptionist to see if Carmen was waiting and had inadvertently been ignored. There was no Carmen. Then 2:30 p.m. came and went. Still no Carmen. My first thought was that I had incorrectly written down the interview time. I checked the e-mail correspondence. All e-mails confirmed a 2:00 p.m. interview. At 2:45 p.m., I dialed the number on Carmen's résumé and left a voicemail message. Still no Carmen. About an hour later—3:45 p.m.—the front desk receptionist called and informed me that Carmen had arrived.

By that time, I had decided that if Carmen could not tell time, she certainly could not work for our station. I walked down to meet her and professionally inform her that she was no longer being considered for the position. I had no intention of investing time with her—no intention of interviewing her.

As I turned the corner toward the front desk, I saw an attractive woman blotting the tracks of dried tears from her cheeks. She saw me and quickly tucked away the tissue, reached out her very shaky hand, and smiled softly. "I am so sorry for being late," she said. "My car was just in a major accident, and I had to wait for the police and ambulance to come. Then I had to get a cab." I escorted her to the conference room, made sure she was physically okay, got her some water, and we talked.

I ended up hiring her. In fact, in the course of my career, I hired Carmen for three separate jobs at three different companies. Carmen's entrance told me she was dedicated, genuine, caring, and human.

I have never forgotten Carmen's arrival that first day I met her. And Robin's first soggy entrance—oh, that's indelibly carved into my mind. And then, of course, there's Duke—confident Duke—who took control wherever he went. And Sam. He knew intrinsically who to play with and who to bark at.

I'll never forget them, and I'll never forget what I learned from them. Was it their genuineness? Their tenacity? Their confidence? Their intuition? Yes.

Lesson 6:

Always Greet People

Before anything, make a genuine connection with people, and you'll make them feel like they matter.

I always said my father could have run for mayor in any town he ever visited. He always greeted people in a way that made them feel good about themselves, and that ultimately made him memorable. Even if he did not know their names, he made them feel like he remembered them. He always smiled at them, made great eye contact, and worked on making a connection with them. There is an art to greeting people. Dogs have perfected that art.

Leave your house for five minutes, walk back in, and see what your dog does. You will be greeted by your furry friend as if you had just returned from a long journey. Cynics say it is because dogs have no sense of time. But I believe dogs just understand (like my father did) that greeting people in the right way will always make you memorable. (I guess you could also say that people who greet poorly will also be remembered.)

Her name was Daisy. She was an old, overweight, white Bichon Frise who belonged to our older, next-door neighbors. My son referred to her as the sausage dog because she did, indeed, look like a very overstuffed sausage with fur. To our neighbors, she was their little sweetheart, but to the rest of the world, she was a snarky, mean-spirited, rotund ball of ill-temperedness.

Once we had acquired two Schnoodles, our neighbors thought it would be great to organize playdates for all the dogs. They would drop Daisy off at our back gate, and she would make her roly-poly way across the yard to our back patio and up to our French doors. Then she would wedge herself through the small doggie door and come into our house. Once in, she stood at the back door to see who was in the room. Our Schnoodles, Fay and Sam, ignored her. If she saw me, she waddled over to my feet, cowered, and usually peed on the floor. If Daisy spotted our son Michael or my husband Robin first, she growled in a mean, show-your-old-tartar-stained-teeth, I'll-eat-you-up-and-add-your-flesh-to-my-already-sausage-like-body tone. Daisy was not fond of men. Daisy was not a good greeter.

Neighbor-organized play dates continued for quite some time, and then the worst possible thing happened. Our neighbors were going to be out of town for two weeks and trusted no one but us with sausage-dog Daisy. In a moment's notice, we became her home away from home, her surrogate family. Her human parents brought over a five-pound bag of Daisy's special food and her kennel (two sizes too small), along with her leash and the phone number for her vet. Daisy was ours for two whole weeks.

Week one: Daisy came out of her kennel when her break-fast bowl was full, gobbled down her food in seconds, and then raced to the doggie door. She wedged her body through the small opening, barely made it to the patio, and relieved herself right there. In her haste to return to her kennel before anyone saw her, she would accidentally step in her patio pee and poop and bring some of it back in the house through the doggie door. Week one: many baths in the utility room sink and thoroughly washing her kennel, her kennel blankets, the patio, and our floors.

Week two: Michael, a natural animal whisperer, was convinced he could get Daisy to like him and curb the snarly growling. With human food in hand, he coaxed Daisy out of her kennel just long enough for her to grab the treat from his hand and return like a bolt of lightning to the kennel. He tried bacon next. Daisy stayed out of her kennel somewhat longer (probably looking for a random speck of bacon Michael may have dropped).

Finally, Michael coaxed her out and actually got to hold her. It was then that he decided she needed to discover the grass outside (versus the patio). So he opened the door, carried Daisy lovingly in his arms, and placed her in the backyard. Once her feet hit the green grass and the smell of chlorophyll filled her nose, she bolted for the doggie door, literally flying into the air. She quickly found her kennel and refused to leave it.

When company came and Daisy heard male voices, she greeted them with louder-than-usual growls. When anyone other than I approached her kennel, they, too, were greeted with ferocious growls. So for a couple days, I fed Daisy with my hands and carefully inspected the living room for any trace that she was secretly getting out and relieving herself. I found no traces. Before our neighbors returned home, I popped the clamps on the kennel and forced Daisy to get some air. I shimmied the kennel blankets away from her body, laundered them, and shimmied them back under her sausage body. When our neighbors returned, we eagerly handed over what remained of the five pounds of food, the leash, the kennel—and Daisy. As a thank you, our neighbors gave us many more Daisy visits until she finally passed away.

A nother neighbor's dog was named Sunny. Her name was befitting, for Sunny was yellow and full of joy. She was a full-grown Goldendoodle. Her curly, hair-like fur cascaded down her body and shimmered in the light when she strutted. Sunny loved old people, young people, children, the UPS man, the garbage men, and my son Michael, who happened to be rather fond of the teenage girl who lived in Sunny's house. Sunny also came to stay with us on more than one occasion.

When Sunny first saw you, she scurried toward you at race-car speed, stopping short of colliding with you. She immediately sat back on her haunches and handed you her paw. Often, she tilted her head, tongue hanging out to the side, which made her appear to be smiling. Sunny was pure canine love. She just made you smile when she greeted you. Sunny then found her canine profession as a personal greeter. She attended advanced training and became a comfort dog for the local hospitals, senior retirement homes, and schools. After all, everyone deserves to be greeted in a way that makes them feel good about themselves.

Michael also became a professional volunteer greeter. He discovered his position as semi-punishment for an outlandish texting bill. Long before unlimited texting was a normal thing on cell phones, texting came with a certain charge per text. Michael was in middle school at the time and had caught the attention of a very flirtatious, aggressive sixth-grade girl who lived with her grandparents. As predictable as grandparents are with their early-to-bed schedules, this unsupervised young lady decided to spend many of her nights texting Michael. Caught somewhere between enjoying all the attention and not wanting to be rude, Michael answered her texts. The outlandish phone bill was $1,600 for one month.

And then my junk yard dog mentality kicked in, and I went off on a three-way corrective measure to pull the choke chain. First, there was the call to the girl's grandparents, which curtailed the texting. Then there was the phone call to the phone company's regional corporate office to negotiate a lower bill. Finally, I needed to teach my little pup Michael the value of $1,600. I proposed it as a volunteer opportunity. Michael needed to find some type of volunteer job and invest enough hours in it that would be equivalent to $1,600—if he had been paid.

At first, Michael opted for building houses at Habitat for Humanity with his friends. "Growl," said this mother dog. "Having a good time with your friends with power tools is not punishment." The thought of six teens doing construction while Robin or I had to be there as adult supervision was not going to cut it. Michael was gently nudged toward personal service hours at church.

After a long, exhaustive search, Michael opted to be a greeter at the church doors on Sunday mornings. I'm sure Michael had already figured out that he would get to see every young, attractive girl his age as they walked in the building. He was the youngest volunteer greeter the church had ever had. At first, he was placed at the side door, but then the church staff realized that Michael not only suited up every Sunday and looked exceptionally handsome, but he was also very person-able and great at greeting. They put Michael at the main door.

I had calculated that the punishment of volunteer service hours would take about four months to complete. Then, the strangest thing happened. Michael really began to enjoy the act of greeting people. People started to seek him out and wait to enter through his door. He shook older men's hands firmly, looking them in the eyes and smiling. He complimented older women and made them feel adored. He made quick connections with other teens his age, and young children *loved* him. In the end, Michael greeted for more than four years. In that time, he learned to always greet people well—and to always opt for the unlimited texting option with your mobile phone carrier.

Greeting people is good for relationships, and relationships are good for business. People like to be greeted. I like to be greeted.

When I walk in my local Sam's Club, Gloria, Sharon, Delores, or Rachel always greet me. They recognize me and ask where Robin is. Donald at Costco always asks me how my family is doing. Catherine is the manager at my local Frost Bank. She smiles at me as I walk through the doors and asks how my consulting business is going. She asks if I am still going to Pilates classes. Pauline hugs me every time I get my hair cut and colored and then hands me a black smock to put on while I wait for my stylist.

In every instance, a connection is made. All of them make me feel like I matter. But no one greets me better than Sam, my little Schnoodle, when I walk through the door from the garage and enter the kitchen. He gently paws at my shins, his tail moving like a metronome. He whimpers his small, expressive whimper that says, "You are home. You have returned to me!"

Lesson 7:

Get Fed Twice A Day

The better-person diet requires you to fill your cup twice a day
—intellectually, emotionally, spiritually, and calorically.

E veryone in my family has always been motivated by food.
We use food to celebrate. We use food to overcome
adversity. We use food to communicate our love for one
another, and we use food as an activity to spend more time
with each other. As our saying goes, whenever two or more of
us are gathered in His name, there is a casserole. It is no
surprise that every dog who has owned me has also been motivated by food.

Fay the Schnoodle first discovered food when she was at
puppy training school. Her trainer wore a canvas carpenter's
apron cinched tightly around her waist. In the two pockets in
front were tiny pieces of hot dog cut in rounds and then into
quarters. Fay discovered quickly that good behavior was easily
rewarded with these morsels of heaven from the hot-dog lady.

"Sit!" Get hot dog reward.

"Stay!" Get hot dog reward.

"Speak!" Get hot dog reward.

"Walk by the left side, immediately sitting when human stops!" Get multiple hot dog rewards.

Although every dog in my life has always had his or her own bowl and special place to eat the kibble in the kitchen (separate from the rest of our eating areas), human mealtime offered an opportunity for our dogs to get additional human morsels, often mistakenly dropped on the floor by ravenous eaters or purposely dropped on the floor by picky eaters. The first family dog we raised in San Antonio was a Golden Retriever named Sunny. During mealtimes she would wedge her girth and fur between the base of the counter and the bar stools in hopes of retrieving carpet samples of dropped food. Then I became more rigorous in my canine feeding schedules. After all, it only made sense that feeding the dog *while* we were eating would delay the incessant begging long enough for all of us to at least consume most of our food in peace.

And so it came to pass that our dogs would be fed twice a day: morning and evening during our breakfast and dinner. The schedule seemed best to accommodate our family's eating schedule since morning and evening were the two times each day that we shared meals sitting at the countertop island. Most dogs will eat as often as you let them, but dogs accustomed to being fed twice a day seem to appreciate the structure. If for no other reason, the anticipation of a morning meal made the morning routine and walk less crazy.

The concept of getting fed twice a day actually serves many purposes. A nutritionist once reminded me that breakfast was the most important meal of the day, simply because it served as the time when your body needed to *break* the *fast* of not having eaten for eight hours or so. I was taught that keeping glycemic blood sugar levels stable made for a happier, healthier body.

For me, breakfast was my favorite time of the day. Breakfast foods were easy to make and always delicious. And the time spent with my family also fed me emotionally. For my dogs, they just knew that breakfast meant something wonderful would be added to their empty bowls and that their family would be joining them in the kitchen for a meal. They too were fed emotionally with pats on the head, scratches of their underbellies, dog hugs, and snout kisses from the kids after breakfast. Once we put our breakfast dishes in the dishwasher, our dogs knew we would be scurrying off by car or school bus, and they would finally be left undisturbed, bellies and hearts full, to begin their morning nap.

Our second feeding of the day meant we were all back home safely and as a family unit once again. Despite home-work, school projects, and open laptops with spreadsheets that needed to be tweaked, our evening meal gave us a chance to share our day with each other. In anticipation of dinner, Sunny would sit near her bowl in the kitchen, almost pointing at the dark void in the bottom of it. I often saw her follow our dance-like movements around the kitchen floor as we all synchronized getting plates out, silverware placed, and water glasses filled. Dinner was organized and predetermined (thanks to all the practice I had during my single-mother years), and everyone helped get it ready and on the table. Then we filled Sunny's bowl.

We said a blessing, and then we shared our food and what-ever was on our minds. Nighttime meals involved conversation. Each person told the antics of their day. We consumed ques-tions and newly learned facts acquired from the classroom or the school bus. We chewed on local events, political events, and stories from the office. Someone often asked the dreaded ques-tion, "What did you do today to make yourself proud?" And we all devoured the answer, listening attentively.

Once Robin joined our family, the kids delighted in playing the dinner game of stump Robin and worked hard in an effort to come up with some trivia question or unknown factoid they could ask him in an effort to stump his vast intelligence and steel-trap-like mind of useless information. Getting fed intellectually gave everyone a voice and a chance to be heard.

As we ate and talked and laughed, Sunny watched us, her head following the conversation like a Ping Pong ball. She got up off her haunches when the volume rose with childlike laughter, almost as if she understood the joke or pun. Then, after dinner, Kimmy and Michael took Sunny outside or in the living room and played rough with her. They hid her toys, played fetch, and wrestled with her. Sunny was also getting fed intellectually.

Throughout my career, the act of being fed twice a day was not necessarily the act of consuming food. I, like most of the busy working class, skipped meals to cram in more work, and somehow there was never enough time. Lunches were a pack of peanuts eaten at my desk so I could be on a conference call, or I'd sneak a piece of candy out of the candy jar on my credenza so I could work through lunch and finish the report.

However, twice daily, I made sure time was set aside to feed myself intellectually, emotionally, and spiritually. Having my cup filled twice a day recharged my internal and mental batteries. I would learn something new. I'd send a note to someone who was on my mind. I would call my mother or sister. I'd take a 15-minute recovery break and walk around the block or drive to the mall and watch people. No matter the activity, I got fed twice a day, and it made me a better person, a better manager, and a better employee.

The kids are grown now and live as far away as two beings can. I'm the only human early riser in my home now, and morning mealtime is often just me and Sam for breakfast as Robin sleeps. Sam waits in anticipation as I fill his bowl. Age has spoiled both of us, and Sam gets moist food mixed into his kibble. I microwave an egg and hit the Keurig to make one single cup of coffee. Times have changed, but morning still is my emotional feeding time. I hold my Sam and stroke him gently. He is older now, but he still craves my human touches as much as I enjoy giving them.

Evening meals are still shared around the countertop. Robin and I work together out of our home office all day, so our intellectual feeding time is perpetual. Occasionally, Kimmy or Michael calls during mealtime, and with speaker phone on, we bombard our caller with life questions. The getting-fed-twice-a-day cycle continues.

Lesson 8:

Serve Your Master

In order to serve your master, you have to respect the person.
If you can't respect the person, respect their title.

At the beginning of this *Surviving in a Dog Eat Dog World* guide, I said I have been owned by six dogs and eight companies in my lifetime. For me, ownership has always been a choice for dogs and companies. However, serving a master requires a mantra.

There was a study published in *Forbes* that projected that 65 percent of all employees would give up a raise if it meant their boss would be fired. The thought of nearly two-thirds of the US workforce hating their bosses so much that they would literally give money to see them gone is incomprehensible to me. I was raised with a Puritan work ethic that required you to respect a position of authority, even if you couldn't or didn't respect the person. For that reason, I placed loyalty high above all in the home and in the office.

If you have ever raised a dog, you understand the loyalty

that grows with each day. Once a dog becomes part of your family, a pecking order is established, and an alpha dog emerges. In my family, the alpha dog was always my dad. (Let me be clear, my mother wore the *capri* pants in our family with her beauty, brains, and brawn, but to the pets and daughters who lived in the house, Dad was clearly in charge.)

Bonnie and Clyde (as we named them) were two full-grown Doberman Pinschers that literally appeared one day coming down the mountain toward my childhood home in Phoenix, Arizona. My dad insisted they must have been lost or abandoned since they showed up partially dehydrated with tender paws from the desert terrain and the mountain preserve near the back of our home. Dad posted signs, ran newspaper ads, and did everything he could to find their rightful owners, to no avail.

After a few weeks, Dad allowed them to become part of our family, and we got to officially name them Bonnie and Clyde. Both appeared to be purebred Dobermans, ears clipped, tails bobbed. Bonnie was red with dark brown eyebrows and perfect markings. She had never been spayed. Clyde stood five or six inches taller than Bonnie and was the traditional black and tan. Clyde's size alone made him gangster-movie scary. Not knowing their upbringing and the fact that Clyde would sometimes growl (baring his teeth) when we came near his bowl, his ball, or Bonnie, Dad chose to take them down to his auction lot. They instantly became watch dogs.

Dogs are funny creatures. Having had a family prior to ours, obvious by the grooming of their ears and tails, Bonnie and Clyde must have realized that fate had led them to my father. So they settled in as watchers over the smaller vehicle lot on the southeast corner of the auction office property. Clyde showed signs of aggression on occasion but must have known Dad was his source of food and sustenance. Bonnie learned to be docile, submissively giving total authority to Dad. Both learned to crave Dad's attention and affection and grew comfortable in their new surroundings. After a few months, we were blessed with a litter of Doberman puppies.

In the northeast auction lot was the office and Duke, German Shepherd Duke, the retired Chicago police dog who reigned. Duke was Dad's favorite dog hands down. They shared a chemistry, a bond of love and total man-dog thing. Duke was stern and regal and fierce, but when Dad was around, he was puppy-like mush. Dad was his alpha dog, his master, and Duke was perfectly fine with that.

One day, some vehicles got moved, and the chain-length fence that separated the northeast auction lot from the southeast auction lot was exposed. Bonnie and Clyde could now see Duke. Maybe it was seeing Dad and Duke engaged in their man-dog time together, or maybe it was just Clyde trying to be the alpha male, but Clyde did not like Duke. While Dad was there in the lot with Duke, nothing happened, but sometime in the night when the auction lot was closed and Dad was at home, one of the dogs dug a hole under the chain link fence, and Clyde and Duke came after each other.

After all, you can only serve one master, and in Clyde's dog-mind, he was the alpha dog, not Duke and certainly not Dad. The neighbors heard the commotion and called Dad at home. Dad rushed down to the auction lot and found Duke pretty torn up and Clyde in worse shape. Both dogs were taken to the animal hospital to be stitched up. For some reason, Clyde survived. Duke needed to be put down. Deep down inside, Dad never could bring himself to forgive Clyde, and Clyde clearly could never bring himself to serve his master. After Duke's death, Dad found Clyde, Bonnie, and all the puppies a new home.

Duke had remained loyal to his master until the day he left my father.

Loyalty. It is a gift.

My children's educational environment applauded and rewarded the alpha mentality. Students were praised for their strong personalities and leadership—both in the classroom and on the playground. From the time Kimmy and Michael entered elementary school, they were taught that they could be anything and do anything. And it seemed like everyone got a trophy. Everyone was a winner. Everyone was in charge.

The hierarchy of authority got muddied even more as parents easily threatened teachers for hurting their children's feelings or not allowing them to be expressive inside the classroom. Today, my children represent a generation of empowerment, self-assuredness, and strong wills—individuals who have grown up believing they have the power to change the world.

How is it then that I can ask this generation, these individuals, to respect authority, be loyal to a company, and serve their masters? How can I tell them that being loyal does not mean they are a doormat? Can I get it across to them that they can be confident enough to remain strong and yet be happy to serve? Respecting authority does not show weakness; it demonstrates strength.

When you respect authority and relinquish power to one who has earned it or has been given the title of authority, you gain their respect. In a society where everyone feels like they are in charge, who wins when everyone is jockeying for position or fighting for power? Like Clyde and Duke, everyone is after each other's throat, and someone will lose.

Serving your master is a skill you must learn. It must become part of the very fabric of your being. In life, business, or relationships, loyalty is the glue that binds people together.

Someone has to be in charge. Someone must call the shots. Someone must make the hard decisions. Someone must lead. It is our duty as employees, as partners, as spouses to allow masters to lead. If you can't respect the person, respect the title. Serve your masters well, and they will respond to you with loyalty to the very end.

Lesson 9:

Don't Bite The Hand That Feed You

If you pick up a starving dog and make him prosperous, he will not bite you.

This is the principal difference between dog and man.

—*Mark Twain*

I have never been bitten by a dog. I have been scratched by many cats, but never have I had a dog aggressively break my skin. I believe a well-loved dog has no reason to bite its master. At least mine did not. Why should they? My dogs were always fed, groomed, walked, played with, and given shelter—not to mention loved. They had no need to bite.

Occasionally, when you try to touch our Schnoodle Sam's legs or feet, he will nip at you, but he will not bite. It's the Schnauzer part of him that just doesn't like having his feet touched. Touch them, and the old grumpy fur man comes out. Sam will quickly pull his feet back close to his body and growl. Unfortunately, our Sam is height-challenged, which makes his need for feet protection all the more necessary. His short, stocky legs do well to support his frame but aren't great for fast running or jumping.

On two separate occasions, Sam has endured surgery to permanently fix a torn cranial cruciate ligament in his knee (same as the ACL in humans), once for each back leg. The surgery further halted his jumping and running abilities. So, our Sam has gone beyond the realm of Schnauzer feet sensitivity to downright overly protective of his legs and feet. But Sam doesn't bite the hand that feeds him.

I have often wondered what would happen if our Sam inadvertently had bitten someone. The likelihood is low since Sam is missing four teeth on the bottom of his mouth. According to our vet, the missing teeth are unfortunately a result of his age. In addition, Sam has had two molars surgically removed due to an unfortunate broken teeth incident involving a chew bone. Even with missing teeth, bionic knees, short stocky legs, and an inability to jump well, Sam is our small but mighty alarm system. He barks a lot. I am sure it is because seeing the world at ankle and calf level is most likely scary. However, Sam's barking serves as a real deterrent to potential passersby and makes him less pettable. Less petting means less chances of someone touching his legs and feet. So, Sam does not try to defend me by biting. More often than not, Sam is the fearful one, which requires me to pick him up and protect him from stranger danger.

In the business realm, I have never bitten the hand that fed me. I have always prided myself on being grateful and being a good steward of my people, my clients, and my company's resources. To me, employment was a privilege, not a right, and all the elements that come with a good job (health benefits, parking, time off, life and disability insurance, continuing education, 401k, company stock) were perks. That is why I am forever surprised when employees bite the hand that feeds them, especially on their way out the door.

Then, there was Sylvia. I inherited Sylvia as part of my sales team when I returned to television sales management in Texas. Sylvia was a B player based on her skills, but she had been at the station for enough years that she felt comfortable. As other sales reps came and went, Sylvia's account list grew. Each new account assigned to her increased her income significantly, so by the time I arrived as her new manager, she was making A player income with little effort.

I have discovered that every new manager brings out a sense of fear in existing employees. I am sure that with my tenacious style, need to have systems, and desire for accountability, I was a threat to Sylvia. The first change I made was to get rid of the archaic pencil and paper sales call sign-out sheet and instead link everyone's Outlook calendars so all appointments could be easily seen, tracked, and documented. Sharing her calendar was beyond threatening to Sylvia. I am sure she felt that by doing this, everyone would know where she was all day and how she was utilizing her time. Sylvia did eventually comply, but only partially. She gave access to her Outlook calendar but marked just about every appointment as private. I felt the first tooth sink into my hand ever so slightly.

Next, I naturally desired to have sales calls with the team so I could get up to speed quickly with the advertisers behind our revenue stream. Sylvia reluctantly took me to see a local advertising agency. Unbeknownst to Sylvia, I had worked with the agency principal for dozens of years and had been an integral part of the agency's success from the start. Sylvia told me that the purpose of the meeting was simply to say hello, but when we arrived, the agency principal was expecting us to present an in-depth proposal for one of the agency's larger accounts. The reunion quickly turned into a bloodletting by the agency. I felt the grip on my hand get tighter as the teeth closed in.

The final bite came a little over a month after that. It was the days between Christmas and New Year's Day. There was a lot of unused vacation time that employees had to take, and we were operating with a skeleton crew in the sales department. What should have been a slow time turned into a frantic time as clients and agencies raced to negotiate and place their annual advertising schedules for the upcoming year. Most of my day was spent covering my vacationing team's accounts. Days were long, and often there was no break from the chaos.

As I was juggling too many balls to count, Sylvia was secretly downloading client information and revenue history and remaking client folders. The last day of the week, Sylvia did not show up for work. Instead, she sent an e-mail to my boss and resigned from her position to accept a position with our biggest competitor. Prior to sending the e-mail, she had completely cleaned out her desk drawers. Every piece of client history, every order, every note had been removed. On her desk was a stack of new manila folders, all perfectly labeled with account names. Inside each one was a typed sheet with just the client contact name, address, e-mail address, and phone number. Sylvia had left, and in the process, she had not only bitten the hand that fed her, but she had chewed it off.

In our career mentoring, we have a saying: "It is better to build a bridge than to burn it." Biting the hand that feeds you is not only the worst kind of wound, but it completely burns up the bridge, which may never be rebuilt. Usually, the bite does not heal. It festers and often contaminates the entire area. What may have been a personal attempt at getting even quickly becomes a hostile betrayal, an unexpected deceit, and downright theft, especially with non-competes.

A biting dog is a big deal. Dog bites often result in legal ramifications that involve animal control, civil court, or even criminal court. Just like a biting dog, employees who bite the hand that feeds them never work out. I have witnessed personal relationships crumble, employers seek remuneration from former employees, former employees get blackballed from future jobs, and the biter of the hand endure years of great personal drama because of their actions. An employee who bites the hand of their employer is also a grave reflection on the employer. Once I psychologically got my head around Sylvia's actual bite, I became hyper-focused on the *why* behind the bite. Could I have anticipated the behavior? Had I contributed in some way to her desire to bite? Could steps be put in place to ensure that future employees don't leave the organization feeling that biting the hand that fed them is necessary, let alone an acceptable behavior? Was there a way to screen out those disloyal employees in the pre-hiring process?

Once the bite from Sylvia healed, her reputation in the marketplace began to precede her. Within a short time, Sylvia felt compelled to leave her new job and seek employment elsewhere. At that point, I received a phone call from a potential employer asking for a reference. I did not give details; I did not open up the wound. Instead, I politely declined and said that I was not *comfortable* providing a reference. There was a catharsis-like healing and self-satisfaction in knowing that my lack of comments was powerful. Before you ready yourself to draw blood and grab hold of anyone's hand with clenched teeth, remind yourself that your master has indeed fed you, groomed you for the role you are currently playing, allowed you to play in his or her sandbox, and given you an opportunity to play at all.

A s for our Sam, despite all the ferocious barking, thankfully he has never bitten anyone. I can only imagine how my feelings toward Sam might change if he bit me or someone else. Although he is my beloved fur-child, surely I would approach him with apprehension and caution if I knew he were a biter. I would avoid connecting Sam with people if I suspected that the outcome might result in injury. No longer would Sam be free to roam around the house or yard when others were visiting. I would always anticipate the worst and shield others from him. Our social Sam, ruler of his domain, would be banished to live a people-less life.

Biting changes everything.

Don't bite the hand that feeds you.

Lesson 10:

It's Better To Be Unleashed Than Led

You can lead with reins or spurs.
   Both will get you there.

That's the the management expression I use often—you can lead with reins or spurs. There are two types of employees, two types of spouses, and two types of children. There are the spur people—those you have to poke and prod and give the proverbial kick in the side to get them to do what you want. And then there are the reins people—those you have to rein in, pull on their choke chain a little, or point their nose in the right direction to get results. As a mother, manager, and wife, I prefer to use reins over spurs any day.

   Dogs know this. They understand that it is far better to be unleashed than to be led. Just this morning while I was walking Sam, I proved my theory. San Antonio has a leash law. All animals on public streets must be leashed. With collar on, extendable leash affixed, Sam and I left the house as the sun was coming up. No sooner did I open the garage door to begin our walk than Sam took off running toward the street until his expandable leash no longer had any slack. His leash became a rigid tightrope attached to his collar. The speed at which Sam can determine he is out of leash does not exceed the speed at which he can race out of the house, run through the garage, and race toward the end of the driveway.

Then it happens—that horrible, fur-ball-like coughing noise that sounds like an old man has lodged a piece of bread in his throat and needs someone to desperately clear it before he chokes. Then comes the nasal wheezing, that guttural sound of Sam trying to get enough air into his lungs to keep himself going. To passersby, I am strangling Sam, but I know if I take a few steps toward him, the leash will loosen up. Then he will get a few soft pats to his back by my loving hand, followed by a few playful words of encouragement, and Sam will right himself and begin walking again. By now, at age 13 and a half, Sam clearly understands the expandable-leash-has-an-expandable-limit game, but he manages to choke himself anyway every morning. Even when I use the traditional leather lead, Sam attempts to outrun the length of it. Sam just knows that it's better to be unleashed than to be led.

When I was at Clear Channel, I hired an assistant. She came with glowing reviews and even a reference from a prominent US senator from Texas. Her name was Jodie, and she was smart and well educated. She had the most beautiful smile with perfectly white, straight teeth. She could light up a room and was ideal for our small but mighty corporate marketing department. What I liked best about Jodie was her gregarious personality and authentic laugh. It just made you feel happy. She showed all the signs of being a good hire, and with her outgoing personality and stellar references, I just knew she would be a self-starter, a real go-getter, a non-stop ball of productivity.

Then our department got crazy busy. There were only four of us, but the workload was enough for a dozen. Suddenly, Jodie was not such a great hire because she required constant direction. I had to precisely spell out every task for her. She had to have exact directions for every responsibility. Jodie needed to be led, but all I needed was for her to do her job. As the rest of our team found themselves drowning in work, Jodie sat at her desk and played on the computer. When confronted, she replied, "No one has anything for me to do."

"Jodie," I said, "we all have things for you to do. You are responsible for all expense reports, all incoming and outgoing mail, and all incoming phone calls. And we really need help on bids for printing." She looked at me as if I were a Cyclops with one eye in the middle of my forehead.

"Just tell me what you need me to do," she said. That day, I came to the conclusion that Jodie needed to be led to do her job. Unfortunately for her, I needed someone who was unleashed and running free—someone I may even have to rein in once in a while.

Ask any employment recruiter, and they will tell you that *self-starter* is usually on the top of hiring managers' lists of key traits. Finding individuals who aren't afraid to take ownership, who problem-solve and identify solutions, who take on additional responsibility without complaining, and can be counted on to complete the project on their own, all within the deadline, is key in today's business climate. But proclaiming you are a self-starter on a résumé is far different than exhibiting those traits on the job. I think of the student who raises his hand and begs the teacher to let him answer before the question has even been read. A self-starter works effectively without regularly being told what to do.

Not everyone is born a self-starter. Unleashing people who

would rather be leashed is difficult. But it can be done. The same goes for dogs. When dogs allow you to lead them, they have either been trained by best-in-show trainers or have some reason to be submissive. Every dog (and kid) I have ever had in my life preferred to be free. I have never had to tell my dogs (or children) that they needed to eat. I have never had to tell my dogs (or children) that they needed to sleep. And I have never had to tell my dogs (or children) that they should be playing. They just automatically did all those things. (Cleaning up after themselves or picking up toys off the floor was another story.)

In our neighborhood, we have a homeowner's association that enforces laws, rules, and codes. One of the biggest complaints from neighbors is unleashed dogs. That became a particularly testy issue when our neighbor Terry moved in with his two Pit Bulls, Bella and Max. Terry's dogs were gorgeous, well behaved, and perfectly mannered. Terry invested much time in their training and often allowed the dogs to be off leash outside in his front yard while he was doing yard work. Bella and Max would lie in the driveway, enjoying the sunshine as they watched Terry. At his command, the dogs would come, heel, and respond directly to him. Occasionally, they greeted a neighbor with a bark or two, but Terry quickly stopped that with just a voice command to Bella and Max. Only a few non-dog neighbors complained. The homeowner's association responded quickly that it was Terry's yard, and neither the animals nor their owner had broken any homeowners' association rules.

Then Terry decided to walk his dogs, unleashed, around the block. Terry walked, and Bella and Max tagged along behind Terry's heels and obeyed every one of his commands. They strutted side by side like two well trained soldiers. But someone in the neighborhood made a formal complaint that Terry was not only breaking San Antonio City code but was also in violation of the homeowners' policy that required all animals to be on a leash. Neighbors sent e-mails, made phone calls, made enemies, and hung up leash law posters.

Terry reacted with diplomacy. Keeping with the letter of the law, both Bella and Max are now leashed when they go on their neighborhood walks. But here's the funny thing: Bella and Max hold their own leashes in their mouths as they proudly stroll around the neighborhood behind Terry's heels and still obeying his every command. Here's the point they are probably trying to make: It is so much better to be unleashed (even if you have to be leashed) than to be led.

Lesson 11:

Getting Stroked Once in a While is a Good Thing

"People will forget what you said, people will forget what you did, but people will never forget how you made them feel."

—*Maya Angelou*

When teaching people how to get a job, I often use the expression, "You have to scratch them where they itch." It is my way of telling job seekers that they need to find a prospective employer's "ooh-aww" spot in order to fill a job niche or identify whatever it is that is keeping them up at night. As a visual mnemonic, I often rub my back on the closest chair I can find and then raise my right leg slightly and shake it uncontrollably. The visual usually makes everyone laugh but also makes a great point. Scratch any dog on their belly, and you will undoubtedly discover their "ooh-aww" spot. The dog will arch its back, and one leg will quiver in ecstasy. As long as you are willing to scratch, your dog will allow you to do so. Move your hand away from the animal, and often his head will follow you. His wet nose will nudge you ever so slightly as if to say, "Don't stop!"

Every dog (and person) in my family has always loved to be scratched. My daughter Kimmy still loves to have her head scratched. Maybe it's the feeling of fingernails wrapping around her long tight curls that gives her pleasure, or maybe it's just leaning into *mom* on the couch, head on my lap, and my hands nudging her head ever so slightly that signifies maternal love to her. My son Michael liked having his back scratched and getting foot rubs, but his favorite thing was when I made him close his eyes, and then I rubbed his temples.

As a child, I loved when someone did the old nursery rhyme with hand motions on my back—"Big X, little dot. Question mark right on the spot." Somehow, the "little breeze, little squeeze" always gave me the chills.

Physical touch is a necessity. Scientists have proved that babies who are touched after birth have more advanced childhood development and recognition of self. Preemies who are touched gently early on can actually be compensated for missed sensory experiences received in late gestation. Then it is no wonder that stroking a dog not only pleases the dog immensely but pleases the person as well. I could go on for pages about the effects of petting animals and lowering heart rate and blood pressure, but instead, I return to the real basis for this chapter: getting stroked once in a while is a good thing. But my point is that non-physical stroking can be equally as important in development and pleasure. Don't believe me? Say something nice to someone and see what happens.

In my world, there are joy-germs and fun-suckers. Joy-germs are those people who fill a room with glee, happiness, and positivity. They are the shine in sunshine. Fun-suckers are just that—they literally suck the fun right out of the room with their negativity, self-absorbed personas, boring personalities, and miserable outlook on life.

I pride myself on being a joy-germ. Every day, I strive to find good in people and offer up positive, cheerful words of encouragement. In the back of my mind, I can hear my mother say, "If you can't say something nice, don't say anything at all." in her Southern accent. Mom was right, and so was Edward in *Pretty Woman* when he uttered the famous line, "I think we need some major sucking up."

I was promoted to be a national sales manager when I was still in Central New York. The job required me to travel extensively to 14 rep offices around the country to call on major advertising agencies. In addition, I had to be in Manhattan about every third week. That left Kimmy and Michael alone with their father or, during longer trips, with my mom and dad who would come from Arizona to Cazenovia, New York, to help.

During that time, I worked for a phenomenal leader, Ed, who always put his employees first. Sensing the stress my travel had on my family, Ed called me into his office. "I have arranged for you to have an account at Kirby's" (Kirby's was a locally owned seafood and steak house that literally was on my drive home.) "I want you to have your family use it when you are out of town or whenever you like. The tab is already taken care of." I was stunned and flattered, first that my family had access to really good free food, but more importantly that I worked for someone who appreciated me enough to take care of me, my stomach, and my family!

Through the years, Ed personified the act of stroking his employees. He purchased a red carpet for the front door of the station and had a plaque made and placed above the door that said, "Through these doors go our most important assets—our people." Daily, Ed would hold up our success with adoration.

He left handwritten notes for the staff and made everyone feel like they truly mattered. The station flourished, and people worked harder just to make Ed proud.

To some, stroking one's ego with words and acts of kindness may be sucking up. But to me, it has always been a fantastic tool in leadership, diplomacy, child-rearing, and self-actualized happiness. Using words or acts of kindness to make people feel good about themselves brings out the best in people. Everyone wants and needs to feel special.

Teenage years are trying years for both parents and teens. Somewhere in the struggle to be half adult and half child, my children needed to know that they were okay, that they were loved, and that they were full of purpose. It was mid-November, and Kimmy's 13th birthday was fast approaching. Her birthday always fell two weeks after her younger brother's birthday, three weeks after Halloween, and a week before Thanksgiving. It also fell during mid-terms when all her teachers felt the need to cram in every major test and assignment before Thanksgiving break. What should have been a celebration of her soon turned into a pity party of self-loathing. Michael stood clear of her volatile explosive outbursts. My personality and big dog persona fed into them.

Had Schnoodle Fay been able to talk, I am sure she would have communicated to Kimmy how great she was in all of her 13-year-old hormonal glory. I am sure Fay would have whispered praises in her ears as she licked the tears off her face. But Schnoodle Fay could not speak in compound-complex sentences, so that is how the "What I Love about You" box started.

For Kimmy's 13th birthday, she received a small metal box. Inside, handwritten on tiny strips of colored paper, were 13 things I loved about her. Each notation was carefully crafted, perfectly penned, one for each year she had been alive, and now available for her to open and read when she felt the world was against her and when she needed to know she was loved. There was nothing over-the-top about the statements. They were true, genuine, and perfectly "Kimmy." But what these magic little notes held was the soft stroke of a mother's heart, available anytime life got unfair. I have continued to send a new "What I Love about You" note yearly to both of my children on their birthdays. They both still have their boxes, open them, and read the notes inside every time they need to get stroked.

As for me, I have Sam to stroke me when I need to be stroked. Sam the Schnoodle became an only fur-child when his sister Fay became critically ill and had to be put to sleep. This horrific event happened on the same day my mother was diagnosed with esophageal cancer.

It was a dark day in my life. Returning home from saying goodbye to Fay was sad. I remember the sky being gray like my heart. A slight mist of rain dotted the windshield. It made the heavens look like they were crying. Getting out of the car, I walked slowly through the garage and opened the door that led into the house.

There was Sam, his knob of a tail moving so fast that I thought he might actually propel himself into the air like a helicopter. His short, squatty legs, barely able to support his stocky body, were trying so hard to jump up to greet my legs that he almost toppled over onto his back. He whimpered playfully in a tone that seemed foreign to me. Had he actually been able to speak, his words would have greeted me with sheer unapologetic gladness. I reached down and picked up my little black dog, and his body quivered with delight as he licked the tears of sadness off my cheeks. Sam knew. Sam responded as any loving canine joy-germ would. Sam stroked my heart.

G etting stroked once in a while is a very good thing. Pets get it. They know that a playful rub against your leg lets you know you are appreciated and acknowledged. Sam's perfectly placed tender lick on my hand reminds me that I am his—just like an unexpected soft kiss on the forehead from my husband Robin reminds me that I am his soul mate and the person he still wants to be married to.

Hallmark owned the feel-good market for years with its precisely written, sometimes flowery greeting cards. Today, we are quick to swipe our thumbs up emoji or place the bright red heart next to a text, Instagram post, or Facebook message as if to offer instant recognition and a "well done" to those we care about. Pinterest offers a potpourri of lunch box note examples, all easily replicated so no child goes to school without a mom making them feel special.

Getting stroked professionally is a little more challenging. Not only has the business environment changed, but the political correctness of everything from structured, templated performance appraisals and reviews to the open office architecture of cubicles does not allow managers to easily single out individuals with the recognition and compliments most employees crave. The old-fashioned employee of the month plaque barely exists anymore. Instead, companies work hard to create a fair and equitable work environment where no employee feels slighted.

As a manager, I also yearned to be stroked in many of my work environments. Recognition was rarely given from the top. Wins were company-wide wins. In my last corporate position, I remember the shocked look on my boss's face when I asked during a performance review if I was doing a good job. His answer was curt. "Of course you are. I gave you a 4 overall on the 1 to 5 scale, and nobody gets a 5." As if a 4 were enough to fill my tank with precisely the number of accolades required to accelerate my productivity through the next year! I left that job.

Stroking employees should not be hard. It is as simple as a handwritten thank you note placed on a chair. It is a sticky note that says, "Wow, you amaze me!" It's a voicemail that says, "I really appreciate all you are doing." I purchased a helium tank just so I could attach balloons to the chairs of co-workers. I kept a file folder full of stickers in my desk so I could acknowledge small victories, and I sent real cards to employees' homes using real, old fashioned mail. Most of all, I used positive affirmation to acknowledge correct behavior (or improved behavior). For every ataboy I did not receive, I doled out two. I became a joy-germ.

I have often wondered if my actions affected others. Clearly, productivity was affected, but were there long-term benefits to all this stroking? One Christmas, I received an e-mail from a former employee. In it was a photo of a handwritten note I had attached to a basket of homemade Thanksgiving baked goods I had made for everyone on my team that year. The note was a personal "why I am thankful for you this Thanksgiving" note. The photo showed that he had tied the now discolored note to a branch on his Christmas tree. In the e-mail, he said that note was the greatest gift he had ever received. My heart was full. Getting stroked every once in a while is a good thing.

Lesson 12:

Don't Be Afraid to Use Your Voice

The only way to find your voice is to use it.

—*Austin Kleon*

My entire family is loud and raucous. We take turns talking over each other in a way that is orchestrated harmony. We are not shy. We tell stories. We sometimes have no filter, and we are extremely dogmatic. Very rarely does anyone in our tribe have a problem expressing their opinions. We love language and relish good uses of puns and plays on words. We make a contest of it.

My first child, Kimmy, uttered her first words at nine months. She was singing by her first birthday. Finding her voice was never a problem. Michael, child number two, had a beautiful speaking voice that could melt anyone's heart (especially his Gram's), and we ironically discovered he had a perfect-pitch second tenor singing voice when he tried out for a high school musical (on a bet) and got a solo. It is no wonder that in all this vocal talent, my oldest sister, Dawn, inherited a singing dog.

Dawn was the first in our family to move to Texas. I was working in Central New York at a CBS television station when she and her husband Mike were both relocated to Seguin, Texas, with Motorola. Texas was a new adventure for all of us. Dawn and Mike searched for a house that would allow them to experience all that was rural Texas. They ended up buying a house outside the small city of Seguin (about an hour northeast of San Antonio.) It included about 14 acres of land and a beautiful view of the Guadalupe River.

The people who sold them the house made it clear that Tick, an elderly Blue Hound dog, came with the property. Tick had proven before that when relocated, he would undoubtedly find his way back to his original house. That was how the sellers acquired him, and that was how my sister got him. Tick was a free gift with purchase. Tick epitomized Texas. He was rugged, dusty, and smelled like the outdoors. His lanky body was the color of the land, and he almost creaked when he walked. You could see his ribs when he stretched, and his long floppy ears slapped his face as he meandered across the porch. He was a hunting dog who regularly rewarded the master of the house with various rodents and fowl that he proudly killed as he scavenged the property.

Dawn and Mike's new home in Seguin was breathtaking. It gave my parents from Phoenix, Arizona, and my two kids and me an opportunity to escape city life and experience the natural beauty of Texas. So we visited often.

The first time my father met Tick, they became instant friends. There was something about this old hound dog that made my father laugh. Dad would throw sticks, and Tick would retrieve them, his loose skin flapping like a flag in the wind as he ran back with the stick in his mouth. Tick and my father were buddies, both of them the salt of the earth, both weathered and worn but still active and willing to earn their keep. The first night at Dawn's was beautiful. The air smelled fresh and clean; the stars that peppered the sky were magnificent. Later, a few clouds gathered and brought some much-needed rain. My dad commented on how well he would sleep with the sound of rain hitting the house's tin roof.

It was heaven until about midnight. Tick had just come home from his final scavenger hunt for the night. He raised his long neck toward the sky and let out the most heinous howl you will ever hear. The screech filled the night air and bounced off the openness. The sound was something between tires screeching in anticipation of a major automobile collision and a hurt child screaming in agony. Lights came on immediately in the bedroom where my father and mother had been sleeping. Dad opened his window and yelled at Tick to hush. Maybe it was the sound of my father's voice that reminded Tick of their newfound friendship. Maybe Dad's words sounded like praise to him. But each time Dad yelled at him, Tick answered with a hound-like singing voice that was strong and powerful. The more Dad yelled, the louder Tick got. Not a lot of sleep was had that night.

Tick sang every night. He had been singing for years. Just as Tick was never about to leave his homestead, he was also not about to give up his voice. He had something to say, and he was darn sure he was going to make everyone listen.

Teaching my children to use their voices came easily in my household. As I said before, we are a family with few if any filters. However, I have found that for some people, finding the courage to speak their minds can be challenging. I have shared the story of Tick with many of my employees. It is a great reminder that we all have a voice, and what we say matters. In order to be heard, sometimes we have to be loud. Sometimes we need to howl a little to get people's attention. And then we shouldn't be afraid to keep on howling until we are understood. Other times, we might want to howl more quietly.

Lindsay was a childhood friend of my daughter Kimmy. She was an attractive girl, but more often than not, she made herself almost disappear when she was in a room. Her long, ash-blonde hair curved around the sides of her face and literally hid her beautiful smile. When she spoke, it was in hushed tones, and the constant guilt-ridden "I'm sorry" statement often came out of her mouth. Lindsay spent the night with Kimmy often, and as they went through their middle school and high school years, Lindsay became a permanent fixture in our household. She tagged behind Kimmy like a puppy. She was Kimmy's shadow.

In fact, Lindsay was like beige wallpaper. You rarely noticed her unless you were looking for her. She just blended into the background. It wasn't until Lindsay began to search for colleges that we discovered Lindsay indeed had a voice. An essay she wrote for the University of Texas in Austin admissions department literally shook Kimmy's world. Lindsay, in all her reservation and quietness, had asked Kimmy to read her essay for one final edit before she sent in her application.

The essay began with the same posturing and hopefulness of most college essays. The prompt was to write about something that had influenced her life. Within the first two paragraphs, we met Lindsay and began to understand the heart of this beige wallpaper young woman. As the sentences flowed, Lindsay unfolded a lifetime of living with alcoholism—an alcoholic mother caught in a disease of destruction and her parents' failed marriage as a result of substance abuse. Then it was her mother's failed remarriage to a man Lindsay despised and the always present need to protect her younger brother at all costs from their mother and her abusive life. It was a family with severe depression, poverty, and anger—lots of anger. Lindsay's powerful words poured out onto the pages like a raging ocean, swallowing Kimmy's heart up in the current.

In our mundane home, Lindsay had found refuge and a little bit of solitude. Being with our family had given her the ability to face her uncomfortable past and put her demons down on paper. Sharing it with the university's admissions staff, people she did not know, was easy. But sharing it with her best friend took a voice of courage unlike any voice Lindsay had ever had.

Lindsay was accepted to the University of Texas and majored in radio, television, and film. She went on to finish her Master's degree and attend seminary where she is working on a Ph.D in religious counseling. Lindsay found the love of her life, married him, and moved to a small town in west Texas. Once she had mustered up the courage to find her own voice, she dedicated her life to teaching others to find theirs. Even today, Lindsay and Kimmy have scheduled weekly phone calls. Hearing Lindsay's voice every Sunday fills my daughter's heart with hope and bravery.

A few months ago, Schnoodle Sam started a very peculiar behavior. For some unexplained reason, at around 7:45 each evening, when Robin and I were sitting comfortably on the couch reliving our day, Sam jumped down from the couch, stood in front of us, and barked. It was not the I-need-to-be-fed bark or the take-me-for-a-walk bark. It was a loud, non-stop, get-your-attention bark. The tossing of the random toy toward Sam did not end the raucous behavior. The walk to the treat jar and the subsequent treat merely curtailed Sam's voice for the time it took him to gobble up the small morsel. Clearly,

Sam had something to say. We continued on with the game of charades until we finally discovered what it was.

People are the same way. Once they discover their voice, they have strength. As parents, we encourage our children to use their words, especially when hysteria sets in and uncontrollable tears and tantrums follow. But adults are faced with the reality that Mom is no longer there to encourage them to verbalize their needs and desires, let alone their feelings.

In the corporate world, companies struggle with communication. It is one of the main reasons consultants like my husband and I stay employed. Suggestion boxes are strategically placed around offices. At times, leadership microscopically examines the few suggestions in the boxes to determine precisely who wrote the suggestion before figuring out how to fix the identified problems. Discrete, anonymous, toll-free, company-wide hotlines are put in place for employees to call when they feel they have been treated unfairly or want to report a problem. In more than two decades, working for three publicly traded companies, I have witnessed failed anonymity every time. What started as a brave soul mustering enough courage to make a call in the first place quickly turned into numerous closed-door meetings with Human Resources. In all cases, the reported misconduct or problem was swiftly reviewed, but not before everyone in the building knew exactly who was behind the call and the closed doors.

How, then, can we encourage people to use their voices? It reminds of when my pre-teen daughter Kimmy screamed at the top of her lungs at her brother and me from the top of the stairs. That was followed by a harsh, purposeful slam of her bedroom door. Without hesitation, I marched up the stairs, removed the pins from the door hinges, took off her bedroom door, and carried it downstairs straight into the garage. The door pins remained in my possession for quite some time. Because of her inappropriate outburst, she had lost her privacy. With her room wide open, her brother proceeded to dart in and out freely. Within hours, I heard laughter from upstairs. Then I heard playing and singing. By that evening, the open-door concept had resulted in open communication.

Although I have never physically removed the door from any of my offices, I have since incorporated an open-door policy. From my first day in a workplace, I have encouraged employees to use their voices. An open door indicated that I was accessible. I even turned my desk and conference table so I was forced to look directly at whoever entered my office, not from over the top of a computer screen. Was the solution perfect? No, but with encouragement, team members felt safe and uttered their ideas, concerns, thoughts, and opinions. Everyone has a voice. When properly encouraged, they will find it and use it. It gives a person an unexplained power and strength that no one can snuff out.

Even Schnoodle Sam found a way to use his voice. After weeks of his unexplained evening barking, we discovered that he was trying to tell us that he wanted to go to sleep, in our room, on our bed. Being height-challenged, he could not jump up on the bed. Once he used his voice and we paid close enough attention to what he was telling us, he got what he was asking for. And that is really all anyone wants.

Lesson 13:

Learn How To Play Ball With The Big Dogs

Size, stature, breeding, and where you came from don't really matter. What is important is being authentic. Love what you do and be comfortable with who you are.

Growing up, we had Chihuahuas. My older sister Susie got Pancho, a small, tan, male Chihuahua, as a birthday present. He was purebred and had perfect markings. He also was photogenic and allowed Susie to dress him up in doll clothes for pictures. Pancho was a good pet. However, he had a way of sneaking out of the gate and running down the street toward any female dog that was in heat. As word got out to other Chihuahua owners that photogenic Pancho had an urge to procreate, Susie conned my parents into allowing her to farm him out for stud services. Susie was only 11 or 12 years old at the time and didn't know the financial potential of her photogenic Chihuahua stud service. So instead of money, she opted for the pick of the litter. In a very short time, our Chihuahua family grew to include a dog for each of my sisters and me. There were Pancho, Blanco, Gomer Pyle, and my Chihuahua, Archie Bunker.

Under normal circumstances, small dogs—Chihuahuas in particular—tend to maneuver carefully in a big dog environment. Ours did not. In fact, I am sure none of our Chihuahuas ever realized they were small in stature. Even when confronted with Trixie, the German Shepherd next door, Pancho, Blanco, Gomer Pyle, and Archie Bunker held their own.

When I was barely 30 years old, I was managing a sales department for a CBS television station in Syracuse, New York that was owned by Meredith Corporation. Our TV station was in the smallest market in the group. At the time, Meredith, best known for their magazines like Better Homes and Gardens and Ladies Home Journal, had TV stations in big markets such as Phoenix, Orlando, Portland, Kansas City, and Pittsburgh. Phil Jones was president of the Broadcast Division and had been a long-time close personal friend of Ed, the Syracuse station's vice president and general manager.

On one particular day, I headed into my office at the normal time, only to be told by Ed's executive assistant that Phil Jones was coming to town and Ed was on his way to the airport to pick him up. A memo quickly went out to our entire department alerting everyone to tidy up their workspaces and get ready for a corporate visit. In my eyes, Phil was a big dog, the biggest dog in our company.

Phil arrived and immediately poked his head into my office. "Today," he said. "I'd like to meet some of our clients. Who's going on sales calls? I think I'll just ride along." Salespeople have personality quirks that make them great at what they do. I had learned that my team seldom liked to get senior management involved unless they really had to, and I knew the last thing my salespeople wanted to do was feel like they were under the microscope in front of a client—with corporate watching. A corporate visit was a career tightrope. I had heard too many stories over the years about the bad consequences that came out of not-so-stellar corporate encounters.

I needed to quickly choreograph perfect meetings that had the potential of making everyone look good. "Phil," I said, "give me 20 minutes, and I'll have a schedule for you." I called a few of our bigger local clients, confirmed times with each salesperson that handled the accounts, and raced to get the entire day filled with quality meetings that could enthrall our clients without costing the reputation of my people. After all, it's not every day that a corporate president comes to town. I pulled my car up under the awning in front of the building. Phil got in the passenger's seat, and the salesperson rode in the back. Off we went on our career make-it-or-break-it day of sales calls.

When playing with the big dogs, I have learned that size, stature, breeding, and where you came from don't really matter. What is important is being authentic, loving what you do, and being comfortable with who you are. The rest of the day was filled with laughter, singing along with the radio in the car, funny stories told with our clients, funny stories told about our clients, and stops for good food along the way. Phil got to relive his glory days as a TV salesperson, and we all got to go along for the ride.

That day, Phil became our station's biggest champion and my favorite corporate big dog.

Introducing the United States to HD radio gave me another opportunity to play ball with the big dogs. Shortly after being hired to the corporate team at Clear Channel, I was told I would be working with the team to launch HD radio. At the time, it was surmised that HD radio would be the second coming for the radio industry. I was asked to work with engineers, our innovation team, the FCC, and other broadcast industry leaders.

One day, the president called me into his office to be part of an HD launch phone call with other radio owners, group heads, and executives. At first, I was a little intimidated to hear the names of well known individuals that headed up the likes of CBS Radio, Emmis, Entercom, Cumulus, and Cox. The names had been etched into my head as broadcast leaders. Mark Mays from Clear Channel initiated the call. I sat next to him with my notepad and pen ready to scribe what I believed would be history-making words of wisdom.

At first, the noise from the conference line sounded as if everyone were talking at once, only to be interrupted by the occasional outburst of laughter as this all-male phone group volleyed spurs at each other. Then Mark reeled in the conversation and began discussing the important matters of HD radio and how it should be rolled out. I had an overwhelming uh-oh feeling as the conversation coasted gently into revenue potential and funding. Let me state that I am not an attorney, but I have had enough law classes and enough experience managing companies to know that when the conversation moves toward the potential threat of antitrust and price-fixing, an attorney should be present. At that point, I tore out a sheet of paper from my notebook and wrote these words: "We should have an attorney on this call!" Mark looked down at my note and nodded his head in affirmation. I am not sure who on the call he interrupted, but he apologized to this group of broadcasting legends and asked for the call to be rescheduled.

HD radio never really changed the country. But working on the project made this small dog—this very small but mighty Chihuahua—confident enough to not only play ball with the big dogs but take the ball and run with it.

Lesson 14:

Always Strive For Best In Show

We are the champions.
  We are the champions.
  No time for losers
  'Cause we are the champions of the world.

—*Freddie Mercury*

Her name was Gracye. She came to my sister Crystal at a time when Crystal needed a Weimaraner puppy in her life. California bred, born, and raised; she was as picturesque as any William Wegman photo. Her silver-grey coat was as soft as velveteen, and her eyes made your heart melt. They were a cross between sadness and frivolity, depending on from which angle you looked at her. Grayce was an energetic, high-strung puppy, devouring any chew toy she came in contact with and leaving trails of commotion behind her wherever she went. Crystal loved Grayce, and at the strong direction of her best friend's husband (who happened to be Grayce's veterinarian),

Grayce (and Crystal) were encouraged to attend dog obedience classes.

Crystal found a handler for Grayce, who quickly mastered basic obedience. Next, Grayce got ready for confirmation and soon mastered all the steps necessary to compete in an AKC event. With her handler, Grayce was the essence of beauty, brains, and obedience. She exemplified her breed with honor and, well, grace! Grayce seemed to enjoy all the attention. Show after show, she racked up ribbons and awards. She was stunning when she was being judged. In the ring, she was Best in Show.

Out of the ring was a different story. Grayce became Damien, spawn of Satan, when she was at home and Crystal was at work. Her evilness and trickery consisted of opening jars of peanut butter left in the kitchen cabinet, somehow physically unscrewing them and devouring the entire contents. That resulted in all food items being placed in the refrigerator or the oven. Nothing was off limits to Grayce. In one incident, she ate the arm of an $8,000 leather sofa. Crystal's designer leather shoes disappeared, pillows turned into scattered fluff across the floor, and the incessant barking caused neighbors to complain and call the police.

When Saturday came, it was show time again. Grayce and her handler strutted across the greens with confidence and ease. Event after event, Grayce almost seemed to smile when her name was called and she achieved another ribbon.

What is it about being told we are champions? I think it makes us even greater than we ever thought we could be. My husband and I took an assessment one time, and I found out that his "love language" was affirmation. Simply telling Robin that the meal he made was spectacular or that he had just completed a task perfectly fueled his soul.

Over the years, I have been in many disagreements with corporate over money, especially when they declared that it was a save-all-end-all for motivating salespeople. Money, I believe, does not motivate most salespeople. I believe it is a yardstick used to measure performance. Money is the byproduct of a successful sales career. First, salespeople must be good at their craft. Then, the money happens. For me, money was not the save-all-end-all. It was the win. For others, it was the sales process or the cat and mouse game. Regardless, I have never employed a single individual who did not stretch their abilities further for me than when I held them up as best in show.

Fiesta is a big deal for San Antonio. With three parades and literally hundreds of official Fiesta events, it is a celebration of the city's rich and diverse culture and heritage. Fiesta has become an annual "party with a purpose," ultimately helping raise funds for San Antonio organizations and nonprofits. In addition, Fiesta serves as the largest tourist opportunity for the city and the Riverwalk with all the local tourism creating massive revenue. This potential revenue sparked the interest of our local San Antonio ABC television station. Televising the Fiesta parades live could create a new revenue stream. But first, we had to make sure we sold all the Fiesta sponsorships. Money was not going to get everyone to stop what they were doing and focus on this new opportunity. Instead, we needed a way to make people feel like they were the best.

Contests have existed for as long as there have been sales teams, and the local sales Fiesta sales contest served to be the motivational push we needed. There are these very odd traditional eggs called *cascarones* that are symbolically used for Hispanic festivities. Hollowed out eggs are washed and dyed or painted in bright Fiesta colors. Then the eggs are filled with fine, colorful confetti. Once filled, a small piece of brightly colored tissue paper is glued over the top of the egg to encase it. Alone, they are quite pretty, but the simple act of cracking cascarones creates all the fun. People hold the eggs in their hands and lightly smash them on top of an unsuspecting victim's head. The fine confetti goes everywhere as it makes its way from the top of their head to the ground.

Now what could be more fun than salespeople having the opportunity to prove they are the best by earning cascarone eggs? The more Fiesta opportunities they sold, the more eggs they had to crack over the heads of their competitive team-mates. The eggs were stuffed with confetti as well as tiny notes and small prizes (movie tickets, grocery gift cards, lottery tickets, and more). The low-budget contest became the most successful sales venture to date. Nothing shouts Best in Show better than confetti.

My children react the same to affirmation. I am no Dr. Spock, but Kimmy was potty trained using a calendar, star stickers, and a chance to earn enough of them to get a new book. Michael went through the same process, but he earned the toy of his choice. Bribery? No. Just a lesson in human self-worth and a chance to be told that you are a champion.

When Michael was in middle school, he had a group of close friends: Ty, Chad, Cody, Ryan, and Joey. More often than not, the boys were with each other before school, during school, and after school. They were great kids and seemed to bring out the best in each other. However, some of the boys, including Michael, were much better at their studies than the others.

"Mom," Michael asked. "If I make straight A's this nine weeks, can we do something special?" Having won a sizable gift card at a fundraiser that day, my answer surprised him. "Michael, if you get straight A's, we can go out to Ruth Chris

Steakhouse. You can order anything you want. And any of your friends who get straight A's can come, too!" Nothing motivated growing teen boys more than food, and the thought that we would go to one of the best steakhouses in town spurred them on.

For nine weeks, the boys lifted each other up, cajoled each other, and tutored each other. As the nine-week grading period closed, everyone but Cody had straight A's. The other boys rallied around Cody and put together an ironclad case to present to Robin and me. They wanted their friend to be able to go, too. After all, Cody had almost all A's—only one B.

Then, the dinner night came. One by one, we picked up the boys at their houses. They opened their front doors with suits on, ties tied, and hair somewhat combed. They were dressed like they were going to a funeral rather than a celebration. But as soon as we arrived at the restaurant and were placed in a special private dining area, they loosened their ties, and the celebration began. The restaurant staff was delightful, having been briefed on the reason for our celebration. We ordered from a four-course prix fixe menu, learned which fork went with which course, and everyone got to taste everything from lobster bisque to filet mignon. The wait staff continually filled their Coke glasses and added maraschino cherries on plastic swords. Then came the bounty of desserts! The boys ate, laughed, ate more, and posed for crazy pictures to celebrate their success. Everyone left feeling like a champion.

Watching the boys that night at the restaurant helped me understood why Grayce loved competition so much. It made me see how she could be such a different dog on competition Saturdays when she was declared Best in Show.

It made me understand why rewards work for people and why it's sometimes so important to be declared Best in Show.

After several months of Grayce winning ribbons and more ribbons, Crystal decided to be a responsible pet owner. She took Gracye to the vet to be spayed. One of the requirements to compete in AKC events is that a female dog must not be spayed. So Grayce's show days were over. Did she remember those days of praise and triumph? I hope so.

Lesson 15:

Never Take "No" For An Answer

Would've, could've, should've. They won't get you closer to your goal.

"No!" That's one of the first words my children learned to say with emotion. It's also a word I often used for motherly correction. However, throughout my sales and management life, I have learned not to take no for an answer.

Gracye, the Weimaraner, lived a great life. She was an only fur-child for my sister Crystal and was pampered as if she were a real child. I often said that if there were reincarnation, I wanted to come back as one of my sister's dogs so I would be treated with a love greater than most of us ever experience. Gracye was loved, and still she yearned for more human contact.

Crystal had a demanding job as a clinical pharmacist. Her job took her away from Gracye much of the day. When Grayce was left to herself, her Damian spawn of Satan side came out. She chewed up wallets, reached and consumed any type of food left on any shelf in the pantry, destroyed mail, devoured anything leather, and barked *loudly*. Crystal would return home, see the evidence of Grayce's antics, and attempt to reprimand her with the word *no*. I believe Grayce thought it was some sort of game.

On one occasion, Crystal joined me in New York City while I was there on a business trip. She shopped for expensive items and took in the sites. When she returned to her historic Craftsman home in California, exhausted, she dropped her Tumi leather suitcase, now bulging with gifts and goodies, just inside the front door.

The next day, Crystal went to work and, as always, left Grayce home alone. Maybe it was the smell of the Tumi leather or the expensive bottles of perfume and makeup inside that reminded Grayce of Crystal. Maybe it was the leftover airport snacks tucked deeply inside the inside pocket, or maybe it was just Grayce's curiosity. But Grayce worked all day attacking that Tumi bag, trying to get to the contents. Through her diligent efforts, she physically moved the bag away from the door and completely covered a floor heat register with it. The heat had nowhere to go that day except into the suitcase.

As fate would have it, it was an extremely cold day in Old Torrance, California. The combination of the perfume, the makeup, and the heat somehow started a fire. With the smoke detector blaring, Grayce safely went out the doggie door and was later found perfectly unharmed, barking in the backyard. The fire had partially destroyed the Craftsman home.

"No" just didn't cut it anymore. Grayce had succeeded and gotten what she ultimately wanted—a membership at doggie daycare. While Crystal was at work, she spent the rest of her days playing with other doggie friends and humans at the expensive doggie day spa.

I n sales, I often taught my teams that no doesn't mean no. It just means I haven't asked you correctly or given you enough information to support your decision. In college scholarships, no doesn't mean no. It just means you need to put on your big girl shoes and ask again—or so our Kimmy learned.

Kimmy really wanted to go to Sewanee: The University of the South in Sewanee, Tennessee, for her undergraduate studies. Sewanee offered a great education, beautiful surroundings, and the opportunity to hike, climb, kayak, and celebrate the outdoors. Kimmy had been offered great scholarships from a lot of other schools, including Rhodes College in Memphis just down the road from Sewanee. But Kimmy didn't find Rhodes appealing at all. About the time she needed to make a decision, I was released from my position as vice president of an advertising agency to a new destiny. It wasn't that money was tight; money was non-existent. I was in a desperate job search, and Kimmy had her heart set on Sewanee, a private liberal arts school that came with an annual tuition of more than $56,000. What do you think Kimmy's mother said? An emphatic no!

Nothing is more powerful than a head-strong teenage girl with hormones raging, with a desire to leave home, with a need to go out of state to school, and with a ferocious will to conquer the world. Nothing is more powerful except an out-of-work single mother. Every conversation ended in a shouting match that ended in "No! You are not going to Sewanee." Finally, about a week before early acceptance letters were due back to the myriad of other schools that were throwing money in the form of scholarships at Kimmy and begging her to attend, Kimmy made a phone call. She had heard no for the very last time.

She took her folder of scholarship letters into my bedroom, got on the phone with the head of admissions for Sewanee, and told him that in order for her to consider Sewanee, they needed to match the scholarship offerings she had received from Rhodes, their rival. After all, she was going to be an exceptional student leader at any school she went to, and if Sewanee wanted her to be part of their student body, they needed to step it up. Somewhere in the conversation, she may have mentioned that her mother was a single mom of two children and that her mother had recently lost her job. But a few days later, Kimmy received a scholarship letter from Sewanee offering her more than Rhodes. She accepted and attended Sewanee for all her undergraduate years. Then she went on to Vanderbilt University to earn her master's degree.

Not taking no for an answer has gotten me and my children a lot of things: a home priced below market value (twice), increases in salary, shares of stock over stock options, great deals on numerous cars, upgrades at hotels, free airline tickets, great seats at the theater, and so on and so on. But the best thing I ever got by not taking no for an answer was a blind date with my now husband, Robin.

Missy was one of my sales managers while I was working at an NBC station in San Antonio. Her gravelly voice made her sound like old movies featuring Lauren Bacall or Kathleen Turner. Couple it with her West Texas southern drawl, and Missy would command the room. She was tenacious and salty with her choice of words. She spoke with authority and a flavorful use of cuss words. Rarely did she not get what she wanted. And that is why her desire to set me up with a man caused me so much angst.

Missy's sister's best friend, Mary Lou, was dating Drew, Robin's college fraternity brother. Mary Lou and Drew had met up with Robin at a Southern Methodist University football game in Dallas. The weekend culminated with less football and more drinking, and Mary Lou, after much cajoling, decided that Robin needed to have someone to go out with when he was in San Antonio on business. Somewhere in all the tipsy conversation, Mary Lou remembered me and the time we had met through Missy at a TV station event.

On Monday following the game, Missy literally marched into my office and told me I needed to go out with this man named Robin. Quickly, I dismissed Missy and the idea. About an hour later, Missy returned to my office with more information on Robin. Based on her sister's conversation with Mary Lou, Robin was described as kind, intelligent, fairly nice looking, and divorced for quite some time. And he had a son in high school. Again, I immediately dismissed Missy and the idea of a set-up.

Then there were Missy's third, fourth, and fifth attempts to persuade me to meet Robin. The sixth time Missy approached my open office door, I gave her a tongue-in-cheek verbal warning. "If you come in here one more time and try to set me up, I will fire you." "Fine!" Missy said. "But let me just say that all you do is work and kids and church and work and kids and church. Don't you deserve to have someone at least buy you a good dinner?"

Missy's words had worn me down and managed to cut to the core. I was a few weeks away from turning 40, and at that precise moment, I did deserve to have a kind, intelligent, fairly nice-looking man buy me a good dinner. "Fine, I said, "Give him my number here at work." Missy hesitated. "He's expecting your call. You'll have to call him." She threw a business card down on my desk. A half a dozen phone tags later, I finally spoke to Robin. We scheduled dinner. About five years later, we were married.

The lesson here is to never take no for an answer. Would've, could've, should've won't get you closer to your goal. Be like Missy. Know what you want. Be persistent. See a no turn into a yes.

Lesson 16:

Know How To Hunt

Never give in, never give in, never, never, never, never in nothing, great or small, large or petty never give in except to convictions of honour and good sense.

—*Winston Churchill*

N one of the animals in my family have ever had to hunt for their dinner. The closest thing my dogs have had to hunt for was the bowl of dog food placed on their mat in the kitchen. Most domesticated dogs don't have to hunt, but the art of hunting is a skill that dogs just innately know. People not so much. But it is very important that everyone knows how to hunt.

Fay the Schnoodle was our squirrel patrol dog. Her self-proclaimed purpose in life was to rid the yard of squirrels. From her vantage point on the AstroTurf-covered platform box built so she could go in the small doggie door into the house, Fay would keep us safe. She had keen eyes and could spot one flick of a tail 20 feet up in the oak trees that lined the brick patio in our backyard. Quietly, patiently, she waited until the squirrel maneuvered its way from tree branch to tree branch until it was close to the patio. As the squirrel carefully climbed down the tree trunk, Fay slowly, methodically moved closer, synchronizing her steps to the squirrel's so her motion would not be detected. As the squirrel's front leg touched the patio, Fay took off like a bullet, ears pinned back in the wind. The squirrel quickly turned and jumped up onto the tree trunk, and Fay, with her poodle-like legs, would jump, too, often missing the poor squirrel by mere inches. Then Fay would bark at the squirrel until it meandered back from branch to branch, tree to tree, and into the neighbor's yard.

Fay took her hunting game very seriously. She hunted for squirrels, cats, birds, and the occasional lizard. She never caught anything. It was never about the kill. It was simply about keeping things out of her yard and keeping us safe.

Fay taught me six principles on hunting that I have applied to every deal I have ever made. I have also used them time and time again with sales teams who need to fill their funnels, kids who need to a make decisions about anything—what schools they want to go to, what extracurricular activities they want to join—my spouse when we decide to make a major purchase or where we want to travel, and prospective job seekers.

1. Know what you are hunting and why
2. Have a plan of attack
3. Pay attention to the details
4. Be patient
5. Don't get distracted
6. Never give up

Hunting is indeed a developed skill for humans. It is not taught in college (to my knowledge), but the concept of identifying a goal, having a plan, and sticking to it applies to so many avenues of life.

Every company I have ever worked for or with always needed to fill the funnel with new business opportunities. For some reason, most media companies believed the way to fill the funnel was to hire a lot of young, inexperienced salespeople who would pound the payment and search out new business. The thought, which I imagine some corporate suit based this principle on, was that these inexperienced salespeople did not have any preconceived notions about whether a prospect was good or bad and would call on anyone and everyone. If statistics played true and they called on enough prospects, some of them would turn into clients. Besides, young, inexperienced salespeople could be paid a fraction of what an experienced salesperson was worth.

Year after year, I witnessed the cycle end in disaster. Inexperienced hunters never knew what they were hunting for; they never had a plan of attack, and one of three things always happened:

1. Inexperienced salespeople quit before they ever filled their funnels with enough prospects to generate actual business for the company. The company ended up paying them for their short tenure and had nothing to show for it on the bottom line.

2. The accounts or new business the inexperienced salespeople sold were not viable and never amounted to a lot of revenue. Paying the salespeople's guaranteed salaries or draws quickly became a debt for the company.

3. The accounts or business the inexperienced salespeople sold produced revenue, but the businesses never paid their bills and became a bad debt write-off for the company.

I n order to hunt, you have to know how to hunt. A logical look at the six principles of hunting mentioned previously will revolutionize any hunter. Let's look at them in detail.

1. *Know what you are hunting and why.* Let's face it, we are all in sales. Every day we need to convince someone to do something. Hire me! Buy something from me! Do something for me! Take me out on a date! Promote me! The list is endless. Whether you are selling yourself or a product or service for an employer, you have to know what you are selling. If you don't know what your product is, how can you determine what you are hunting for? Determine that, and you can figure out how to fill your funnel.

2. *Have a plan of attack.* Whether you are a job seeker or a car salesperson, start with the end in mind. In the advertising industry, we always looked at profit margin and closing ratio. How many widgets do you have to sell in order to make a profit? How many customers or people do you have to talk to before one person buys a widget? Simply multiply the number of people you need to talk to by the number of widgets you need to sell in order to reach your goal. That is the number of prospects (or potential customers) you need to hunt for. Your plan is created by taking that number of prospects and dividing it by the number of days or hours you have to devote to hunting. That daily (or hourly) number represents the number of prospects you need to contact, see, or get in front of. Break your hunting down into smaller, more comprehensible goals. That will help you stay on task.
   Commissioned salespeople quickly learn that if they

contact more prospects, they will close more business. More business ultimately means more money in their pockets. Ironically, the more prospects a salesperson gets in contact with, the more confident and comfortable they become with the entire hunting process. Quickly, their improved hunting skills dramatically affect their closing ratios and the amount of their average sale. Everyone makes more money.

3. *Pay attention to the details.* Keep track of your progress. Even Fay the Schnoodle figured out the squirrels' pattern of up the small oak tree, a quick jump to the big oak tree, and onto the roof toward the front yard. So Fay camped out in front of the small oak tree. We humans need to camp out where we, too, can hunt the most. Write stuff down! I am always amazed by people's lack of note keeping skills. Hunting is a lot easier when you document your efforts. CRMs, databases, Excel spreadsheets, calendars, yellow legal pads—they were all created to keep track of details. All that data is powerful. Use it. Retrace your steps. See the patterns. When are you most productive? Is there a type of prospect with which you are most successful? Once you determine your sweet spot, see more of those types.

4. *Be patient.* Stick with the plan. Consistency is key. How many of us have started on a diet, began an exercise program, taken up a new hobby, only to find that months later our clothes are still too tight, the expensive tennis shoes we bought have barely been worn, and our stack of how-to books is in a corner covered with dust? Hunting takes time. When job seekers come to our career transition classes, they start out scared but eager. As the weeks

progress and they have not yet landed a job, they panic and begin to apply for jobs they are totally under- or overqualified for. The result is no job and even more frustration. Once they begin to hunt for prospective employers with a consistent process, document their activity, and stay the course, they always land a job.

5. *Don't get distracted.* Squirrel, nut, ball, flying bird, treat. The distractibility of some dogs has given rise to a multitude of memes. Shiny objects are everywhere. It is easy to let even the faint sound of a ticking clock derail your course. But hunting takes laser-like precision. Stay the course. Stay focused. Set small goals and reward yourself for achieving them. I remember when I placed 10 pennies on the desk of one of my newer hires. The instructions were to essentially play dialing for dollars. Make 10 appointment-setting calls with potential advertisers. Every time a successful call was made, the salesperson put a penny in his pocket. Once all 10 pennies were off the desk, he got to take a break, and we reviewed his efforts. Staring at those pennies kept him on track.

6. *Never give up.* The thing I love most about a good hunting dogs is their never-ceasing desire to hunt until they have captured their prey. Often, their owners must physically make them stand down in order to get them to quit. Humans don't always have that determination. Lack of success sometimes gives rise to an alternative activity. If it's too hard, we just quit. But quitting while hunting will only result in failure and a low sense of self. Winston Churchill said it best: "Never give in."

Hunter Fay enjoyed her squirrel patrol so much that she was given a life-sized, realistic, plush squirrel chew toy with a squeaker. It was her favorite toy. She knew it by the name *squirrel* and would retrieve it on command. At any given time, you would find the plush toy on its side looking so authentic that it appeared dead. Fay would grab it and shake it vigorously from side to side.

One day, on the mat just inside the doggie door, Fay was sitting next to her plush squirrel. She seemed particularly proud, almost regal. I spoke to her and asked if she wanted me to the throw squirrel for her to catch. She got up quickly and excitedly, ready to play. I bent down and grabbed the plush squirrel only to discover that it was not the plush toy squirrel. It was a stiff, real squirrel that was quite dead! I screamed for Robin and my son Michael to come help me remove the rigid carcass from the mat and dispose of it. How gross! Surely Fay did not kill a squirrel almost her size!

After the mat was sterilized with disinfectant and the squirrel properly disposed of, I found out that the yellow Labrador Retriever next door was quite the hunter and had managed to maim this particular squirrel just before it scooted over the fence into our yard. When it landed on the grass at the bottom of our fence, it must have succumbed to its injuries. Once dead, Fay found it and brought it to us through the doggie door.

Remember, Fay's hunting plan was simply to keep things out of her yard and keep us safe. It had just been about the thrill of the hunt. But now Fay had caught something. She was now a hunter—a great hunter! A squirrel patrol dog extraordinaire.

Lesson 17:

Always Get Enough Sleep

When you lie down, you will not be afraid; when you lie down, your sleep will be sweet.

—Proverbs 3:24

Scientists have proved that dogs sleep 12 to 14 hours a day. That makes sleeping a full-time job! It is no wonder they live such great lives. Sleep, eat, play, sleep, eat, sleep. That seems to be the pattern.

When we had our first San Antonio dog Sunny the Golden Retriever—the kids cajoled me into allowing Sunny to have a litter of puppies. Sunny was a purebred Retriever but never came with AKC papers. That was part of the agreement when we got her from her first family. Sunny was healthy, and I (somewhere strategically suspended between single mother guilt and stupidity) allowed myself to succumb to the non-stop begging for puppies. (Later, there will be a full chapter on the art of begging.) One of my managers had a beautiful, large, purebred Golden Retriever male, and suddenly Sunny had her first doggie date. About two months later, we had eight healthy puppies. We were the favorite house in the neighborhood for all the kids.

Golden Retriever puppies, actually any puppies, are the best. There is the silliness that accompanies their not-grown-into-their-bodies-yet legs, the cuddly softness of their fur, the happiness of their tender licks and nibbles, and oh, the puppy breath! Is there really any better smell than puppy breath? But my favorite thing about puppies is the uncontrollable narcoleptic way they can be going full speed and then suddenly conk out and go right to sleep. A puppy might be playing with you, tugging on the rope toy, and then, without hesitation, the puppy's body goes limp, the puppy falls to the ground, and the puppy goes fast asleep. At that moment, you can literally scoop that puppy up in your hands, and its entire being becomes like Jell-O. A sound sleep later, they are ready to go again.

As the puppies got older, Kimmy and Michael would race home from school to play with them in our large backyard. During the day, the puppies were safely kept confined in a large inside kennel in the garage with access to a large dog run next to the house. Once Kimmy and Michael set them free, the puppies explored the sandbox, weaved in and out of the bushes, laid in the sunshine on the concrete half basketball court, and ran in the soft grass. Kimmy and Michael wore the puppies out one by one until they finally collapsed to the ground wherever they were when they ran out of steam. Once all eight puppies were sound asleep, the kids collected them and took them into the garage kennel, placing them on the soft, clean bedding. There they slept peacefully, dreaming their puppy dreams.

I have never had any problem going to sleep. Days have always started early, and work hours have been long. Then there was dinner, helping with kids' homework, kid fun time, laundry, and some e-mails or work to finish from the office. By the time I finally got into bed, I was often asleep before my pupils had a chance to dilate from the lights being turned off. Getting to sleep was not the problem. Getting enough sleep? Well, that is precisely why I included this chapter.

Starting with my teen years, I was a creature of habit, always going to bed a little after 10:30 p.m. and rising rather early. My body, so in sync, rarely required an alarm clock. Even in college, I had 7:40 a.m. classes on my schedule so I would be forced to get up early. It wasn't until I became a mother that I shortened my hours of slumber in order to get everything done that needed to be done. I don't even recall much of my first year of motherhood. Sleep deprivation caused that zombie-like state. As the kids got older, I crammed as many waking hours as I could into each day.

Dogs understand what people don't. Getting a fair amount of sleep promotes good health. The National Sleep Foundation recommends that adults get seven to nine hours of sleep each night. Prolonged sleep deprivation can cause fatigue (been there), clumsiness (already there), weight loss (I would go without sleep for days if that one played out), or weight gain (that explains so much). It can also adversely affect the brain and cognitive function. That one is a big ouch! But as a wife of a husband who has been diagnosed with sleep apnea, I can tell you the reality of this one can be very serious unless it is treated.

I have never met a dog who refused to sleep. Sure, when we first got Schnoodle Fay and then Sam, there was some whimpering at night as the new puppy got acclimated to its new home in its new house with its new people-mates. But dogs just know how to sleep well.

I'll admit it, my dogs have always slept in the house with me and my family. Sam occupies my bed. Although I know many an expert who would balk at a dog joining its human in sleep, there is something quite comforting, soothing, and peaceful knowing that Sam is sleeping quietly. Maybe it's the security aspect of having my dog near me that makes me sleep better. Maybe it's the reality that I trust my dog's hearing far more than I trust my own if something were to go awry. Or perhaps it is that on a cold night, I sure do like the little heater feature that comes with my dog.

Sam has a nighttime routine. Once he is told that it's time to go to bed (now mind you, he could have already been sound asleep for more than an hour on the couch when this nighttime ritual takes place), Sam bolts out the doggie door and literally makes the rounds around the circumference of the backyard, barking loudly. This boisterous display takes about two minutes. I am sure Sam is telling everyone that it is nighttime, it is bedtime, and he and his humans are going to bed. I am also certain he is warning everyone and everything that he is now in charge. His bark warns everyone that he will not tolerate any mischief or unwanted, unwarranted, or unexpected interruptions during his sleep.

Sam returns to the house and makes his way to the left side of the bed. That's my side of the bed. He uses his guttural growl to signal he needs to be picked up. Remember, his short 4-inch legs don't jump well. Sam will not enter the bed from the right side, even if I am not present. In his doggie world, you can only get into bed on the left side. Once on the bed, he finds his pillow, his special toy bear in overalls with rope for legs, and his special blanket at the foot of the bed between Robin's and my side. He circles, rutting around on the pillow, until he has made his perfect nest and then falls down into it.

With rare exception, Sam is still in that exact spot when he awakes in the early morning. Say what you will about sleeping with a dog, dogs know how to get enough sleep. And somehow, I sleep like a baby when Schnoodle Sam is on his special blanket at the foot of my bed.

Dogs teach us just how important sleep is. Who knows, maybe that good night's sleep can make tomorrow just a little bit better.

Lesson 18:

Dream

If you cannot picture yourself doing it, being it, or achieving it, then chances are it will never come to pass.

Schnoodle Sam has a doggie bed in virtually every room. There is a gray one in my office where Sam sits and watches me write. He has a doggie bed in the living room so he can curl up and watch Robin and me watch television or read. There is a doggie bed in our bedroom. It doesn't get used very much since Sam thinks our king-sized bed is his doggie bed. And there are doggie beds in each of the guest rooms upstairs. These only get used when the kids are home or when Sam needs alone time and retreats to the dark quiet. Sam likes his beds.

But so you do not think this crazy dog lady has extravagantly spoiled her pet like a Hollywood reality star, let me clarify. The beds were not all purchased for Sam. We had other dogs and being the fanatic, I am about keeping them clean, they are still in like-new condition and too good to throw away. Besides, I am sure there should be some law against selling used dog beds just like there are US laws against resale shops selling used mattresses due to bed bugs, mites, fleas, or transmittable microbes.

So, Sam has six dog beds. That suits him fine since he is our sleeping dog. Sam has perfected the art of sleeping. Sam is not a curler-upper sleeper. He sleeps on his side, feet straight out in front of him, with his head propped up by the elevated side of the doggie bed. He tries to make his body as long as he can. I am certain this is an energy efficiency thing because Sam's black coat makes him extremely warm-blooded no matter the house temperature or season. On occasion, Sam will roll onto his back with his feet straight in the air, exposing his round belly to the circulating air from the ceiling fan above him.

Once asleep, Sam snores his little dog snores and dreams. I know he is dreaming because his feet quiver ever so slightly, almost like he is trying to run. His snore now changes into a more rapid breathing sound as his mind experiences the delights of his sleepy-time adventures. Sam dreams every time he sleeps. Once awake, he opens his eyes and is happy. There is never any groaning, never any growling. A few stretches and Sam awakes from his dreams, recharged and pleasant. For this reason, I am sure that Sam's dreams are only happy dreams. If he dreams of being chased, it must be from a pretty female dog that yearns for his companionship. If he dreams of searching for food, he must find a cornucopia of delicacies that include hamburger meat, chicken, cheese, and popcorn (Sam's favorites). In his dreams, he is not hurt, never scared, always protected, and loved. Sam knows how to dream.

Humans cannot control their nighttime dreams, at least not this human. However, I have often channeled my inner Sam and taken time to daydream. I have found that daydreaming is an important component of happiness. Spending a couple of minutes in the theater of your mind, dreaming (like Sam) of only happy things, makes you relax, makes you become more self-actualized, and helps you visualize solutions to problems and create new ideas or plans for your future.

In just five short minutes, I can turn away from the phone, the computer, the television, the book, and allow the panoramic movie of my thoughts to take over. In my daydreams, I play out how meetings will go. I practice conversations before the words actually leak out of my mouth for real. I consider scenarios and see successful outcomes. Never do I enter into an important decision or does an event take place without a daydreaming moment when I have predetermined the happy ending in my mind-movie.

Growing up in Phoenix, you know how to swim. If you started your freshman year in a public high school and had not yet mastered basic swimming, you had to learn the basics during required physical education class. I had learned to swim well when I was six or seven years old, so I was transferred from basic swimming to the advanced swimming and diving class.

Diving served to be more of a challenge. I had easily mastered most swimming strokes and basic front dives, but I had always wanted to do a jackknife dive. There was something beautiful about that dive—the way the diver bends at the waist in mid-air, legs straight and together, toes pointed, and then the hands touch the feet. Beautifully, like a butterfly's wings unfolding, the body unfolds to become completely straight. The arms, then the head enter the water in a forward pike dive.

My oldest sister could do them, but I couldn't. I watched other divers. I stood at the edge of the deep end of the public pool and practiced bending at my waist. I practiced my approach and lift of the right leg on the diving board, but I just could never elevate my body enough to get my legs straight, touch my feet, and then open up again before splashing unco-ordinatedly into the water. I remember sitting in Mrs. Eberly's freshman English class daydreaming about this dive. I could picture my sister doing it beautifully. I could still see in my mind my friend Cindy doing the dive during last period's PE class, but I couldn't picture myself doing the dive correctly. I never did master a jackknife, but I learned the power of daydreaming and using the theater of your mind to play out scenarios.

I do not believe that if you can see it, you can do it; however, the opposite is true. If you cannot picture yourself doing it, being it, or achieving it, then chances are it will never come to pass. I worked with a very smart, attractive young woman who had moved from California to Austin, Texas, after working in the entertainment industry in Los Angeles. Then she had moved home to San Antonio. She was in dire need of a job, so I worked with her on packaging herself (her elevator speech, her résumé, her LinkedIn profile, her network, her cover letters, and her social media presence).

We spent a couple of hours practicing her interviewing skills the day before she had a real job interview. We focused on the hard-to-answer questions like: What are your salary requirements? Why is there a gap in your work history? Why did you quit your last job? Then we focused on situational questions and goal-oriented questions. But she stumbled when it came to this one—Where do you see yourself in three to five years? What she really wanted was to be working in the film industry. She had the connections and the door had opened, but timing had delayed the production of the film project, so she needed to work *now* to pay her bills. Her fear at this precise moment was that the potential San Antonio employer might find out that she planned to leave as soon as the film project was back on track.

I interrupted her mid-sentence as she stumbled to answer my three-to-five-years question. I looked at her and said, "I want you to close your eyes and think about where you want to be. Picture yourself at the Oscars. Your dress is couture, black, embellished with rhinestones. It sinks deep down in front. The thin pieces of leather that make up the straps on your designer shoes cut into your feet and pinch the outside of your arches as you walk elegantly, gracefully toward the stage. You swing your hips ever so slightly as you move to masquerade the excited quivering of your legs and arms. Your face, cheeks, and jaw ache from the stretched skin of your ear-to-ear smile that seems glued onto your face. The shine of the lights almost blinds you. Then, hands shaking, you reach for the Oscar." She opened her eyes and said, "Yes, that's where I want to be!" "Then tell them that!" I said. "Stories sell!" She did just that and got the job. Someday, she will be working on the film project. Daydreams do come true.

I have always believed that I am going to win the lottery. My mother was the luckiest woman I have ever known. She could scratch a $2 scratcher and win $50. She did it often, begging anyone to take her to the grocery store when they were in town. On the way home, she would sit in the passenger's seat, scratching the small cardboard tickets. I can close my eyes and still hear the sound of mom's thumbnail scratching against the ticket. I can still smell the crayon-like smell of the small gray shavings that flew all over the seat and floor in the car.

Lottery tickets were my mom's gift of choice. For Christmas, my father always put a lottery ticket in each of our stockings. One Christmas morning, our phone rang. On the other end was my sister Susie calling excitedly from Phoenix. "Mom just scratched her stocking lottery ticket and won $10,000!" Susie shouted. My mom really did win $10,000 off a $5 scratcher that Christmas, and I, too, am going to keep daydreaming about winning the lottery until I actually do win.

In my daydream, I see the invitation that will go out to our immediate family, inviting them to join us for a special soiree. It is there that we will reveal to them the magnitude of their share of the winnings. I have rehearsed the pre-meetings with our attorney and our accountant to create our foundation and set up our trust. I have played out the press conference. Every detail is rehearsed, blocked as though it is a Broadway show. I keep reminding myself that all it takes to win is a dollar and a daydream.

S am wakes from his late afternoon nap. He stretches, curving his chest and face down toward the floor. He approaches the desk where I usually sit and work and eyes his treat can that is strategically placed just out of his reach on the left corner of my desk. He whimpers slightly, directing his pathetic growl toward the can almost as if he were trying to get the can to react to him. He paws toward the can. Sam must have been dreaming about food again.

Lesson 19:

Avoid People That Are Mean To You

Surround yourself with companies, employers, co-workers, colleagues, and friends whom you trust and who give of themselves unconditionally.

For the most part, dogs just like being around people. Occasionally, you may find a dog that cowers around people or just cowers around *certain* people. I have seen this with animals that have been abused, abandoned, or neglected. On Saturdays, before we found our first San Antonio forever pet, I would take the kids to the Humane Society to play with the dogs up for adoption. Kimmy would flock to the dogs who were hyper and jumping up and down in their kennels, almost as if they were shouting, "Pick me! Pick me!" She would ask for their kennels to be opened so she could join them, snuggle with them, and revel in their licks and windshield-wiper tails hitting her body.

Michael would seek out that one dog who was cowering in the back of its cage with its head down and its tail stiffly tucked between its legs. Often, the dog would not make a sound.

Sensing the grim reality of this unadopted pet, Michael approached the animal softly and spoke directly to the animal in his warm-toned voice. Michael is our dog whisperer. Had he not always had his hopes set on building things and later becoming an architect, I believe he would have made a great vet. He has always had this beautiful way of calming down any animal. It's as if they just know he is a good person with a kind heart and a soft side. Once Michael had the attention of an underdog dog, he would begin to caress the dog's coat. After the animal realized that Michael would not hurt him, Michael would touch the dog's neck and face. Within moments, Michael had the misfit canine to the front of the kennel, tail wagging and ready for love and play.

As I watched Michael dog-whisper these forgotten and under loved animals, I often thought of what their plight must have been to make them dislike people so much. Had they been physically abused, malnourished, mistreated, left alone too much, tormented, or simply scared by something horrific? How was it that these forlorn animals knew that Michael was not going to add to their sadness? I believe dogs have a special sixth sense that tells them who to avoid and who to trust. Although our dogs have always loved unconditionally (we will explore that in the next chapter), I have often witnessed dogs who just knew who they could trust and who they should avoid.

When I started in the television business, I had to learn who to trust, and I quickly learned how to play the "avoidance game." I was hired as a commissioned salesperson, selling commercial airtime for WTHV-TV, a CBS station in Central New York. Back then, everything about television was sexy. On-air news personalities were local stars, and the fact that you worked with these stars made you a big deal. Add to the stardom factor the marketing merchandise and tchotchke with the station logo. Mix in some free tickets to events, golf shirts, sweatshirts, and T-shirts. And don't forget the expense account you had for wining and dining clients. And like magic, you became very popular among business owners, advertising buyers, friends, and neighbors. But as a commissioned salesperson, if you didn't sell something, you didn't get paid.

I have always been tenacious; however, one of my early personality traits was that I "niced" people to death. In other words, I was overtly friendly, always trying to be kind, and willing to stop and help anyone at any time. I was like that dog up for adoption, jumping up and down in the cage saying, "Pick me! Pick me!" That's how I met an advertising man by the name of Bill who had been in the marketing business for about 40 years. He represented many big clients but had never really done a lot of business with our particular television station.

As the new sales kid on the block, I was assigned to Bill's advertising agency. Bill could not have seemed nicer. He reminded me of a favorite uncle. He always allowed me to come and present sales ideas and special opportunities to him, but despite my salesmanship and tenacity, unfortunately he never bought anything. Often, he called me and asked if I had lunch plans. I gladly accepted the invitation, eager to have another chance to get in front of him, to position my station and try to sell him an advertising schedule for one of his many large clients. Time and time again, I would leave lunch with no sell, but I always paid the check. When any event of magnitude came to town, Bill always asked me for free tickets, holding up his big clients as the people who had requested them.

One day, I literally got tired, frustrated that I could never get Bill to spend any money with my station. And I needed snow tires for my old Volvo. So, I stopped by one of Bill's "big" accounts, which happened to be the largest tire dealership in our area. Call it fate, call it karma, call it having a sixth sense, but I approached the counter and asked for the manager. The gentleman behind the counter answered that he was not the manager but was the owner of the chain of dealerships.

I introduced myself, and somewhere in the I-need-snow-tires discussion and the I-work-for-WTVH-TV comments, we struck up a conversation. Within minutes, I asked him why he had never tried using television advertising on my station. His answer was flabbergasting. He said he *did* advertise on my station and had been advertising on it for more than five years! He added that Bill created an expensive schedule every month like clockwork.

Just like one of those unadopted, underdog dogs in the kennel, I felt a need to trust this man. Moments later, the tire dealership owner went to his back office and returned with a file folder filled with literally years of advertising agency invoices, all charging him for 30-second commercials on my station that were never actually ordered by Bill and thus never booked at the station. The tire dealership owner had paid Bill tens of thousands of dollars every year for commercials that had never aired and never been accounted for except for the fraudulent invoices he had sent every month to this nice man who was helping me get new snow tires.

As the years have gone by, I've retold the story of Bill and the nice tire man many times, but I have definitely focused more on what unethical advertising agencies can actually get away with. It serves as a great lesson in humanity, in trust, and in the need to always dot our i's and cross our t's. Before I left Central New York, the tire dealership owner became one of my favorite clients. His appreciation and dedication to me overflowed. I became a small part of his family. And my relationship with Bill at the advertising agency grew understandably distant. Although legal actions were never taken, Bill knew that I knew. The unspoken words of my distrust were present in every subsequent meeting. Bill had committed fraud and become a fraud in my eyes. Bill not only lost a client but also lost my respect.

Mean people are everywhere. They're the people who steal your time, your money, and your dignity if you let them. I often categorize these types as suers and claimers. Suers are people who threaten to sue you at the drop of a hat. Claimers are people who think nothing of filing a false claim against their company or even their insurance company. They are those employees who claim that company property is theirs and think nothing of using it for their personal gain or just outright taking it—stealing from the company.

One of my best stories about claimers is about my boss's boss, the vice president and general manager for our TV station. Weekly, we had required sales managers' meetings. As we gathered to discuss revenue and market conditions, my boss's boss began to brag about how he had just gotten two new tires for free that morning. The story he told was that after waking up that morning, he realized the tires on his Mercedes were showing signs of excessive wear. He knew he had hazard insurance on his tires and that the dealership would replace them in the event of a flat due to a road hazard. So he lined up a nail behind each back tire and drove over them.

The nails, of course, punctured both balding tires, which began to lose air and deflate. Before they went completely flat, he drove his Mercedes to the local Mercedes dealership (which happened to be one of the station's larger clients) and told them there was lots of construction around his house and he must have driven over some nails. As he continued with the story, he made it a point to share with us the puzzled comments by the Mercedes serviceman that it was really rare for two tires to both get nail punctures in similar places at the same time. My boss's boss bragged at how he overcame those objections. He ended by saying that the dealership was replacing both tires with new tires for free and had also given him a new Mercedes as a loaner car.

I clearly remember sitting in the office listening to that story of fraud. Here before me was my boss's boss, the leader of our station. His title alone was worthy of respect. I often thought that if he lied about tires, what else was he capable of lying about? My boss's boss may have gotten new tires that day, but he lost my respect.

In sales, there are people who take embellishment to such lengths that it is flat out lying. There are users, cheaters, and cutthroats. Co-workers have changed the start times of important meetings on my calendar so I would look irresponsible by showing up late. Leaders have promised promotions, additional vacation time, personal time off, and reimbursement for out-of-pocket expenses—and magically they have never happened. I have had my ideas and work products stolen by employees who then used them to get new jobs with our competitors.

Once, I even had a boss do a line of cocaine in the passenger's seat of my car as we were driving on the New York State Thruway to Albany. When I confronted him, he said, "You know, at the stroke of a pen, I could change your account list, take away accounts, and change your income." That was in the late 1980s, and hopefully, times have changed. More laws are in place to protect people; however, mean people still exist.

This is not meant to be a diatribe against bad co-workers, unethical employees, or less than stellar bosses. Nor is it meant to be an opportunity to hop on a me-too bandwagon and complain about all the times I have been taken or used by mean people. I write this to let you know that there are mean people everywhere. In business, in life, we all need to develop a sixth sense that tells us when and how to avoid mean people before we turn from feeling useful to feeling used. Age and experience could easily make one cynical. Instead, I have chosen to avoid surrounding myself with mean people. It is a choice I make daily.

That is precisely the lesson here. Chose to avoid mean people. Surround yourself with companies, employers, co-workers, colleagues, and friends whom you trust. These are people who give of themselves unconditionally. Study people. Learn about them. Do your research. Be more perceptive. With social media at our fingertips, it is much easier to discover someone's reputation before you experience it firsthand. And if you happen to be inadvertently confronted by mean people, forgive—but don't forget. Learn from the experience.

I n all my experiences, I could allow myself to be considered an underdog dog. I could feel like the dogs Michael always had a soft spot for in his heart. But I have made a choice. I won't allow myself to be considered an underdog dog waiting for the Michaels of the world to rescue me. I will be known as the misfit who sided with the *good* side of evil. I'll be the *good* dog every time.

Lesson 20:

Love People Unconditionaly

If you practice forgiving unconditionally, you will practice loving unconditionally.

My sister-in-law Melonye rescued a Cavalier King Charles Spaniel that was part of one of the largest puppy mill raids in North Texas. She named her Abby. To see Abby is to see royalty. You will find her perched on Melonye's lap, her soft, round eyes shaded by her long eyelashes that accent her gentle, melting expression. Her lavish chestnut-colored, silky, rich coat cascades down her white legs. She is indeed a precious princess.

However, Abby's life was not always so precious. Abby was a breeder and had been confined to a cage for so long that when she was rescued, she could not walk. Her back legs, lacking the muscle strength necessary to support her own weight, collapsed as she tried to stand. Her body, which had served as a protective cocoon for many litters of puppies, was thin, almost emaciated. She was horrifically underweight and frightfully frail.

From the day she came home to her Fort Worth home, carried in by Melonye's arms, Abby has unconditionally loved Melonye and the others in her household. Abby's love is whole-hearted. She is free now, protected, cherished, and has pushed away the memories of the puppy mill. Abby looks up at Melonye with an adoration that speaks volumes. To describe the bond that Abby has with her people is to describe a baby's first smile upon seeing its mother's face. This unspoken feeling between master and pet is like a storybook romance. This adoration is not limited to this precious pet and the family who rescued her. Unconditional love is simply a dog's nature.

Frankie's love story is similar. I lost my sister Susie more than five years ago. Susie had health and chemical dependency issues that took her life when she was in her early 50s. My other sisters and I had moved Susie from California to Phoenix so she could be closer to our mom and dad. With Susie came her comfort dog, Frankie. He is a small, yellowish-blonde, mixed-breed dog. He got his higher-pitched bark from his Chihuahua genes and looked as though he might have had some Terrier and perhaps Papillon genes as well. He loved Susie, but I often feared that Frankie might have been the target of some of Susie's rage when she was under the influence of a potpourri of prescription drugs and alcohol. At times, Frankie was standoffish and didn't like to be touched or held. He also wouldn't eat food out of bowl. He preferred to eat it out of Susie's hand or off the cold floor. In happy times, Frankie went everywhere with Susie. He sat in the passenger's seat of the car and then in a shopping cart when they went into a store. Frankie was Susie's life, and vice versa.

Susie died in her home. Next to her was Frankie. When my sister Dawn and I arrived at the house, Frankie was visibly upset. People deal with death differently. I can only imagine what the loss of Susie meant to Frankie. Dawn seemed to feel Frankie's grief deeply. As Frankie desperately searched for anything that would provide him some normalcy or comfort, Dawn scooped him up in her arms and quickly took him outside. In all the darkness of this tragedy, Dawn rescued Frankie, and Frankie found Dawn. Together they helped each other through the death of our sister.

To see Frankie today is to see a totally new dog. He has found his spirit. He is joyful and cuddly, and he loves his new forever home in Rio Rico, Arizona. Frankie lost his Susie but found his soul mates in my sister and brother-in-law. He also got his own dog sister, Paprika. Frankie loves them all unconditionally.

People find it hard to love others unconditionally. To love another human being is to allow yourself to be vulnerable. It is putting yourself at risk of being hurt. So, we put up walls and boundaries. We create conditional relationships, and when they become uncomfortable, we toss them to the side.

At the beginning of *Surviving in a Dog Eat Dog World*, I declared that I have been owned by six dogs, owned by two children, and, for all intents and purposes, I have owned two husbands. I have loved all my children and my dogs unconditionally.

As for my husbands, unfortunately, my first marriage ended in divorce. I think a piece of me died during that time of dark upheaval. The void was deep and difficult. There were fights, and there was silence. There was anger, and there was regret. There were attorneys, and there were counselors. Losing a marriage is like losing a part of yourself. To me, the pain of failure trumped the pain of my broken heart.

As a manager, I worked vigilantly to not let my divorced heart shine through at work. Almost like catharsis, I mimed taking off my divorce robe daily when I entered the workplace and replaced it with my professional leadership robe. At that time in my career, it was important that I did not allow my vulnerability as a person to overshadow the leadership persona I had created as a counselor, mentor, and teacher. It wasn't until my assistant noticed that my wedding ring was missing that anyone knew I had divorced my husband. By not allowing myself on a daily basis to grieve openly through the divorce process, I had kept my colleagues from displaying unconditional love to me throughout the painful divorce period. In the end, my actions at work had created walls and could easily have compromised the trust my team had for me as a leader.

Professionally, it is hard to love unconditionally, especially when our personal environment is not filled with unconditional love. I have learned that good managers allow their personal and professional lives to blend in a way that they become human in the eyes of their employees. Showing compassion and unconditional love in the workplace makes work so much easier. After all, whether you like it or not, the people you work with become your family for eight or more hours each day. The more you love them, the easier they are to work with.

Looking back now, I clearly see I did not always love my first spouse unconditionally. My expectations for a happy marriage volleyed somewhere between Nora Roberts and Nora Ephron, and unfortunately, both of them wrote fiction. I have healed now and have come out on the other side of happily ever after. Like Abby and Frankie, I practice unconditional forgiveness so I can practice unconditional love.

Lesson 21:

It's OK To Look At The World In Black and White

There will always be a black-and-white difference between profit and loss, success and failure, right and wrong, good and evil.

I live in living color.

Everything that surrounds me is bright, cheery, bold, and somewhat over-the-top. To look in my closet is to see a sea of fuchsia, turquoise, lime green, bright red, and sunshine yellow. My mother always had this expression: "Be seen and smelled before you enter a room." Those words echoed through my head as a child and an adult, which is why I continue to wear good perfume and bright colors every day.

It used to be understood that dogs could only see in black and white. Today, experts think that dogs may actually see in light yellow, blue, and gray. Regardless, the colors dogs see are not bright. My Schnoodle Sam does not view our perfectly painted purple walls in the arched entryway of our home as anything more than walls. At only 9 inches off the ground, I am sure Sam sees everything as just walls or perhaps shadows not to be bumped into.

Ironically, my colorful self first married a man who discovered as a grown adult that he was color blind. The thought of this discovery makes me shake my head and smile to this day. Imagine going through elementary school and high school without knowing that the colors you were seeing were not the right colors? Surely some kindergarten or first grade teacher must have realized that Ed had color issues when his red balloon picture was not colored in red. As Ed's wife, I shudder to think how many times I asked, "Does this blouse match these pants?" or "Which shade of pink do you like better for Kimmy's room?" Ed went on to become a television news anchor. His nightly conservative wardrobe was perfectly paired (by me) and labeled so the tie, shirt, sport coat, and slacks didn't clash. Ed's world was more than black and white but a little less colorful than mine.

About five years ago, I remember watching a CBS *60 Minutes* story about Chaser, a Border Collie owned by John Pilley. Chaser was one of the smartest dogs in the world. He could identify 1,022 toys by name. On command, Pilley would ask Chaser to find a toy. With 95 percent accuracy, Chaser would identify the toy by shape, by size, and by characteristics, but to my knowledge, not by color. I wanted to meet Chaser. I wanted to watch him pick out toy after toy as instructed by his master. Both master and dog were truly well trained! None of my dogs have ever been so sophisticated and so well trained. My dog's worlds were pretty black and white.

When we had both Schnoodles, Sam and Fay, we coordinated everything from dog bowls to leashes. Fay was a girl, so she got the red leash. Sam was a boy, so he got the black leash.

Fay's collar was pink; Sam's was black. Fay's bed was turquoise; Sam's was brown. Even the couch blankets that the dogs used were color-specific. Despite our best efforts, both dogs really could care less who got what, who laid on what, or who wore what as long as they were fed and walked daily. To Sam and Fay, it was all black and white.

In the mid 1990s, the CBS station I was at in Central New York went through an ownership change. Meredith Corporation sold to Granite Broadcasting Corporation. I had loved working for Meredith. They were a wonderful company with outstanding leadership. Most of the employees were sad to see Meredith sell our station. As the sale came closer to fruition and since I was one of the only senior managers who remained, I took on greater station management roles. The transition was grueling. I had just had my second child and was asked to come back to work just a few weeks after.

Granite was a highly leveraged company and operated on a shoestring. Every penny spent was carefully managed and "make more money" became the daily mantra. Business became harder under Granite's ownership. Our viewership declined since the penny-pinching, cost-cutting measures put in place would not allow us to purchase or produce high-quality programming. As a direct result, our advertising revenue plummeted.

It was 1996, and I was on a weekly conference call with Granite's CEO and its president. "We need more revenue," both demanded, "or something we can give our stakeholders and stockholders to show them we are serious about turning this station around." After discussion with corporate leadership, they decided I needed to terminate my local sales manager, and corporate would hold up this termination as a gauntlet to the stakeholders. It would demonstrate that we were doing what needed to be done to turn the station around.

My local sales manager was a strong leader and very well

respected with the team and our clients. He was a hard worker and had a passion for his people and the station. He had grown up through the ranks as a sales leader and had risen to the call of management when we needed him to do so. He also was smart and from a large family of very good New York attorneys. Terminating him was not right. He had done nothing to warrant being terminated. I had no documentation to justify cause for termination and doing so without cause would put the station in a potentially precarious legal situation. To me, the decision was black and white.

I was not about to put the station in legal jeopardy in order to fire someone who shouldn't be fired in the first place. So I went back to the same two people—the CEO and the president—and stated boldly, "If you want me to terminate my local sales manager, allow me time to first meet with my manager, outline the revenue issues, and then create a performance improvement plan. If it is not successful, that will be the documentation and justification we need to terminate for cause." The CEO quickly saw my predicament and the risk of pulling the trigger without a plan. The president did not. "If you aren't going to get rid of him," the president sarcastically said, "then maybe we should think about getting rid of you."

Words are black and white.

I hung up from the conversation and called a friend of mine in the television business. I flew out that weekend for an interview with the Post Newsweek ABC station in San Antonio. Two weeks later, I moved to Texas.

Despite my colorful self, I have continued to flourish with my black-and-white views of business. Either you make the sell, or you don't. Either you make budget, or you don't.

Either you are dressed for success (in appropriate attire to see clients) or you aren't. Either you are on time or you are late.

Managing in the last 10 years has stretched my black-and-white views into all shades of gray. Millennials came to my department without the necessary skills and training. Our own news department touted that by 2025, three quarters of the US workforce would be Millennials. To me, Millennials proved that I could no longer hire and expect those individuals to hit the ground running. Suddenly, more structured onboarding and real training was necessary. So, I took painstaking efforts to implement formidable onboarding protocol for my new hires and began to reteach basic skills.

Structured office hours became lax, people came and went as they desired, and no one higher up seemed to be watching the office. All I could think of was that all this disruption was costing the owners of my company money, and since I was a stockholder, it was partly my company. One day, I calculated that one employee who was late 10 minutes a day was equivalent to one extra week of paid vacation annually for that employee.

Finally, the ultimate gray area was crossed. During the midlife crisis of the vice president and general manager, office attire became a hodgepodge of anything goes so he could dress more like a tech start-up groupie than a leader of a $58,000,000 television station owned by a conservative, publicly traded parent company. I learned firsthand that I am not a fan of ripped jeans and graphically offensive, worn-out T-shirts, no matter how much they cost.

Until then, I had grown stations, departments, and people with black-and-white principles. I prided myself on being fair. Leadership to me was not about being liked or being cool or being trendy. It was about being respected, and fairness and respect grew hand in hand. Perhaps the pendulum has swung too far. There will always be a black-and-white difference between profit and loss, success and failure, right and wrong, good and evil. I am content to look at the world like a dog does —in black and white. But I may have to wear my rose-colored glasses to do so.

Lesson 22:

Be Easily Trained

Train up a child in the way he should go; and when he is old, he will not depart from it.

—*Proverbs 22:6*

For lack of a better term, Lily is our granddog. She is a purebred Keeshond. She was adopted by our son Michael and his girlfriend Jackie when Michael was finishing up his Bachelor of Architecture degree at Rhode Island School of Design. In spite of my motherly advice—*never* get a dog with a girlfriend and do *not* get a dog until you have graduated, are settled, and know where your job is going to be—Michael got Lily.

If you have never seen a Keeshond, your first reaction will be "Wow! They are beautiful." That will be followed by "Man, they have a lot of fur!" Lily stands about 17 inches tall and weighs about 30 pounds. Sporting two layers of thick silver and black fur, a ruff or fur collar around her neck, and a curled tail of more fur, Lily is beautifully plush yet sturdy. Despite all the fur, she is only a medium-sized dog. Apparently, Keeshonds are related to the German Spitz breed. Regardless of where she came from, most people are utterly intrigued by Lily's pleasant personality and all that fur!

Before Lily, I had never had a granddog. I assumed that the only real responsibility I would have as a grandmother would be to comment on the occasional pictures of Lily and share them with comments on social media. Then Michael got an internship in New York City for the summer, and Jackie decided to quit her job and take a job in Myanmar. Jackie departed for Southeast Asia, and I flew out to Rhode Island to bring Michael's car and Lily back to San Antonio for the summer. Michael agreed to join us on the long drive home and then fly back to New York in time for his internship.

Lily is a cold-weather dog. She likes long walks in the densely wooded forests. She loves walking on the rocky Rhode Island beaches. She loves playing in snow and lying on the creaky, cold hardwood floors that are a mainstay in old houses back East. For the record, there are no densely wooded forests in San Antonio. There are no beaches. There is no snow. As for the hardwood floors, we could accommodate that, but when the average outside summer temperature in San Antonio hovers in the mid-90s to low 100s, cool floors are not enough.

With Michael's SUV packed with everything he didn't want to be stolen while he was away from his apartment in Rhode Island, I attempted to get Lily to jump into the car for our 2,000-plus-mile ride back to Texas. In spite of coaxing, Lily would not attempt the small jump into the back seat.

"Michael," I said in a not-so-pleasant mom voice. "What is her problem?"

"She doesn't like to ride in the car," Michael answered.

"How do you get her to the woods, to the beach, and to the fields of snow so she can run?" I asked sarcastically.

"I shove her in," Michael responded. "She usually just pants until we get where we are going."

The thought of 2,000-plus miles with a panting dog who hated to be in the car made this old lady shake her head in already worn-out patience. This older lady also has older kidneys and needs to stop frequently for bathroom breaks. Of course, that meant that Lily could not stay in the hot car and would need to be picked up and placed on the ground, exercised, and then placed back in the car every time we stopped. That would certainly cause much anticipated angst. That was it! Lily needed to be trained!

The journey to San Antonio would first take us through Maryland where Michael would visit his biological father, Ed. Then we would go through Nashville so Michael could spend time with his sister, Kimmy. And finally, there would be the long, 15-hour drive through Arkansas, East Texas, and home to San Antonio.

As the trip progressed, I learned that Lily had a sensitive stomach and required special food in small amounts at a preferred height in order to aid digestion and keep her from throwing up. I learned that Lily needed to be brushed daily. I discovered that Lily preferred to sleep in her special foam bed. And, as I already knew, Lily hated car rides. The entire time we were in the car, she panted. She panted so much that she drooled profusely and made her blanket soaking wet. She refused to eat and did not want to drink water until we stopped for good for the evening.

"That's it," I said. "Google what to give a dog to calm her down for a car ride." Despite Lily never being given anything but her special food, a small dose of Benadryl made the trip more pleasant for Lily and for me.

San Antonio is hot, and that's coming from someone who grew up in Arizona. I can only imagine what Lily must have thought when the pads of her paws hit the cement in our driveway for the first time. There, Lily met our Schnoodle Sam and learned instantly to bark at him. Then the real training began. Lily was introduced to the doggie door. How Lily managed to wedge all that fur through the small doggie door will always be a puzzle to me. But once Lily discovered she had a large fenced-in backyard at her disposal, she quickly learned how to go in and out the doggie door all day long.

We got Lily a small wading pool. She never really used it, but the birds loved it. And Lily discovered she could bark at birds. Lily was introduced to treats, including chicken breast left over from dinner, bones brought home in doggie bags from some of San Antonio's finest restaurants, and bacon. (Nowhere in the granddog doggie code is it written that this grandmother could not spoil her granddog.) Lily learned to eat out of a regular bowl, and she ate everything without throwing up. She learned to jump into the car and sleep on our bed. And she learned the art of begging. Training Lily to be a spoiled dog took most of the summer.

When Michael finally returned, Lily showed him how much she loved her grandparents and San Antonio. But her destiny was already set, and after one trip to the vet, Michael had what was needed for the ride home. He gave Lily a magic, small sedative—wrapped in cheese, Lily's new favorite morsel—and set out on what would be a semi-tolerated ride back home to Rhode Island.

Whoever said you can't teach an old dog new tricks under-estimated the brilliance of granddogs and the power of grand-parents. There is a proverb that says, "Train up a child in the way he should go; when he is old, he will not depart from it." That applies to fur children, too. To this day, Michael says that the summer in San Antonio was a train wreck that ruined Lily. Personally, I just think Lily likes grandma best.

R eminiscing over time spent with Lily reminds me how magical it would be if we all had a proverbial grandma at our workplace who would teach us new tricks and spoil us with affection and praise. Some companies have tried to do just that. Many have hired in-house trainers. Clear Channel created an entire Clear Channel University for leadership development and sales training. Many of the other companies I worked with either brought in experts for half-day seminars or were willing to send employees (if they asked) to off-site workshops and conferences to explore the newest innovations.

I have found that rarely is there a lack of teachable moments at work. However, there *is* a lack of people who want to be trained. Some of the best advice I ever got was to always keep growing and learning. Today, information is at our fingertips, and technology can make many daily tasks easier. But in order to utilize the technology, we have to be willing to learn the technology.

While I was a sales manager in San Antonio, the corporation invested in Salesforce software for its television sales departments across the country. I was giddy to think that we would have access to a state-of-the-art CRM to manage all our customer (client) data, sales processes, and information. Prior to Salesforce, our television account executives kept track of their own client data (phone numbers, addresses, contact information, personal information like birthdays and spouses' names) on their own systems. Sales proposals were shoved in a manila folder or stored as a PowerPoint or Word document on someone's desktop computer.

There was no quick and easy way to put together a database for marketing purposes or chart the sales funnel. Getting a simple holiday greeting card mailing list was a nightmare. To me, Salesforce was the Holy Grail for a solution. The Salesforce team conducted webinars, sent web links for training materials, and even came on site for the installation. Master data taken from all current sales contracts was downloaded by the IT department, and then each account executive was asked to scrub the information for accuracy and add e-mail addresses, current phone numbers, assistants' names and contact information, and any personal data and sales proposals they had for each of their clients. Sounds simple, right? Yes, if you are a person who is willing to be easily trained and see the potential end result.

But somewhere, lost in the corporate-is-making-us-do-this tone from higher leadership and the yes-this-is-important-but-don't-let-it-take-us-away-from-selling push to make budget, everyone did not complete the Salesforce database of client information and materials. Those who embraced the new system and learned what it could do for them loved it. For those who never bothered, they continue to do what they have always done. Someday it will catch up with them.

I learned that you just can't train the unteachable. And I learned that they all should have been more like Lily.

Lesson 23:

Run Like Someone Left The Gate Open

When the gate (or door) opens, run as fast as you can. Trust that timing is serendipitously perfect. Run!

R unaway Fay, as she was known in our gated community of 90 homes, suffered from all types of anxiety. Had it not been for her poodle-like legs and sleek aerodynamic body, Fay, the anxiety-ridden Schnoodle, might very well have been left to cower in a corner. But given her lean but muscular build, unbridled energy, and small but nimble size, Fay became quite the runner.

When our son Michael first spotted Fay, she was merely a blob of grey fur balled up like a thrown-away tissue in the back of a breeder's kennel. In the same kennel as Fay was her last littermate brother, an energetic, curly, white bundle of excitement jumping enthusiastically up and down to get Michael's attention. For Michael's nine-year-old birthday present, he got to choose a dog.

In our true family-affair fashion, Michael, his older sister Kimmy, her best friend Lindsay, Aunt Crystal visiting from

California, Robin, and I all gathered around the Schnoodle kennel to assist Michael with his selection. Unanimously, we all opted for the friendly, high-spirited, white ball of fluff. Michael opted for the nervous, thrown-away-looking, gray catastrophe of a puppy hiding in the back. The breeder reached in and handed Michael his Fay dog. As we filled out paperwork and received instructions from the Schnoodle lady, Michael held his two-pound ball of nerves closely and safely in his arms. Fay quivered as he stroked her ever so gently.

The ride home was long and quiet. By that time, Michael had wrapped Fay up in the bottom of his T-shirt. I glanced over my shoulder to the back seat to see Michael grinning ear-to-ear as proud as any new father could be. Fay's eyes slowly closed in slumber.

Once home, Michael was instructed to put Fay down in the yard outside the car in case she needed to relieve herself. Fay ever so slowly put one paw in front of the other as if she were testing the cool grass. She found a spot, tinkled, and was immediately scooped back up into Michael's arms. "Michael," I said, "You really need to take her inside and put her down so she can get used to her new home." Reluctantly, Michael obeyed. Then, it happened. Realizing she was an only fur-child and not in the shadow of her white, energetic brother, Fay took off like a bullet. As Michael ran, Fay chased him. Around the sofa they both went. When he changed directions, Fay reversed herself and sprinted to catch up. The faster he ran, the faster she ran, and when he stopped, she fell back onto her haunches, her small gray paws out in front of her, readying herself for the next race. Surely this was not the same cowering gray Schnoodle! Indeed, Fay was home.

The rest of the weekend was spent in exhausting play time. Michael would throw the small rubber ball; Fay would attempt to go find it. Michael would run; Fay would chase him. When he plopped himself on the couch, Fay would jump with all her might to grab hold of the sofa cushion, ultimately hoisting herself up next to him. When Monday came, Fay was placed in the small powder room off the kitchen. At first, a chair was placed in the doorway and a makeshift barrier created with cardboard. Fay whimpered loudly as if to say, "Don't leave me!"

So I chose to come home during lunch to check on Fay and let her out to do her business. I opened the garage door that led into the kitchen and peeked over the cardboard barrier into the powder room. There was no Fay. My heart sank. Could someone have stolen her? Surely she couldn't have disappeared! About the time my panic was setting in, Fay came running across the kitchen floor. I scooped her up. "Where have you been? How did you get out of the bathroom?" I took her outside, loved on her a bit, and returned her to her cozy powder room. No sooner had I turned to go out the door that led to the garage than Fay scaled the cardboard chair barrier and was at my feet. "Guess you are just going to have to have the door closed," I said to the bionic-legged puppy.

Closing the door wasn't the answer. As long as Fay's people were home, Fay was fine. Leave Fay, and she would exercise her superpowers and wreak havoc on the floors, the doors, the couch, everything. Having free reign of the house wasn't the answer, either. And there was a bigger problem. As soon as you returned, Fay would bolt out the door you had opened to come in the house and take off running lightning fast down the street. We spent hours in runaway-Fay escapades. Running, to Fay, represented freedom, and being chased while running was the best game of cat and mouse imaginable to our small, gray Schnoodle with Olympic legs. Quickly, everyone in the neighborhood knew her name and that we had a run-like-the-wind escape dog.

After consulting with our vet, we all agreed that Fay might very well just like to run, and if we provided her with ample running space, she might be more content. The next option was to install a doggie door in the bottom, middle pane of the French doors that led to the back yard. For Fay's size, a small cat door worked perfectly. But there was quite a steep step down from the doggie door to the back patio. So we constructed a box and covered it with AstroTurf. Then we wedged it against the back side of the door. That made it easy for Fay to go in and out and also gave her a perch on which she could sit and be on squirrel patrol. Fay seemed content.

Then, one Saturday, a thunderstorm came, and lightning struck a transformer close to the house. The sound was ferocious, and we discovered that Fay was overwhelmingly afraid of thunder, rain, lightning, and even the beeping sound of the emergency alert system on TV. Anything that remotely hinted at bad weather made Fay run out the doggie door (or any open door she could find) and somehow escape down the street.

We bought Fay a Thundershirt®. We attached chicken wire to the back fence. We buried it and covered it with sod so Fay couldn't dig out. We installed an electric fence around the perimeter of the yard, but Fay learned to scale the fence to avoid it. We attached automatic closures to all the exit doors in the house, but nothing could stop runaway Fay. Another trip to our vet suggested tranquilizers or getting Fay a friend. And that's how we got our second Schnoodle, Sam.

As much as I loathed having to chase after Fay every time she got out and went on one of her running adventures, I appreciated her spirit on these adventures. Fay clearly ran like someone left the gate open. Fay was our free spirit, an adventure waiting to happen. Along the way, Fay (and our family) met everyone in the neighborhood. On two bad-storm occasions when Fay snuck out of our subdivision and headed across town, our family came together in tears and prayer and ended up meeting two lovely families who loved our Fay almost as much as we did.

I have always surmised that Fay felt liberated as she bolted down the road, the wind tucking her ears back against her head and her skinny legs sprinting in sequence. The wind blew the fur on her Schnauzer-like beard back and exposed her snout, making her look like she was smiling. Perhaps she was, not because she was free but because she had a family who would run after her when she ran like someone left the gate open.

When Clear Channel went private and became iHeartMedia, the privatization resulted in downsizing. Along with thousands of others, my entire department and I were eliminated. I found myself chasing after a new job.

Up until that point, jobs had always just come to me. Doors opened, and I walked through. Now, positions I checked out would end up being filled internally, put on hold, or eliminated altogether. The faster and harder I ran after a potential job, the greater the letdown. And many of these companies had once all but begged me to come and work for them.

Frustration set in. At the coaxing of my husband Robin, we began mentoring and volunteering with a career support group to help others learn how to find jobs. The career doors never again opened for me, but the floodgates did. And so I ran. I ran fast through that gate, and we started our own consulting company. Never had I felt freer or more equipped to help others succeed.

A new opportunity had begun. It was not a financial floodgate, but we were okay. The freedom of being independent gave me the ability to take care of our teenage son Michael who had become quite ill. For the first time in my life, I could be a stay-at-home mom when necessary, and right now, it was critically necessary. It was a time of being untethered and unrestrained. There were no fences or electric fences, and someone had left the gate open!

I have always believed in divine intervention, in a higher power calling me, navigating me, using me. When that gate (or door) opens up, run as fast as you can. Trust that your timing is serendipitously perfect. Run like Fay!

Lesson 24:

Know Where Home Is

Home is where one starts from.

—T. S. Eliot

For as long as I have commuted back and forth to work, I have had a routine that allowed me to place mental and spatial boundaries between home and work. No matter what city I lived in or the physical location of my office, I identified a physical place or landmark halfway on my commute that became my dividing line. Once the front of my car crossed that imaginary line, I no longer allowed the stresses of family, home, or children to fill my mind. Instead, I filled my mind with work issues. During the commute home, I did the opposite. Once I crossed the landmark, only thoughts of home flooded my mind and my heart. I instituted this process when I moved to Texas, when I was a single mother of two small children.

My home is indeed my castle. It is my refuge and my sanctuary. To passersby, it is merely an upper middle-class house made of brick with a massively large acorn-shedding oak tree in the front yard. Come too close to the life-sized, fluorescently painted iron men sculptures we named Rod and Art sitting near the mailbox, and Schnoodle Sam will begin to bark ferociously. This is Sam's sanctuary, too, and he will defend and protect it with all his 16-pound might. To any unwanted intruder, this home stuffed with all its kid art, world collections, handmade wood crafts, and yard sale trinkets could very well be 10 pounds of crap in a five-pound bag. But to me, it provides solitude.

I bought this house almost a year after I relocated to Texas. When I first moved to Texas, real estate wasn't moving in Central New York. With no desire to have two mortgages, I rented a two-bedroom unfurnished apartment and moved in with Kimmy and Michael. As winter came and went, heating the abandoned home in New York became costly. Finally, potential renters turned into buyers, and we were financially free to buy a Texas home. Desperate to move, we opted for a nearby home we had been scouting for months. In April, we purchased our two-story abode and moved in the same day.

Owning a home gave Kimmy and Michael their things back. They had all been locked away in wooden crates in a storage locker since our initial move. Owning a home provided streets for bicycles, a real bathtub, stairs to decorate for the holidays, a fireplace, and a private fenced-in backyard perfect for a dog. Then came the constant begging, nagging, deal-making, and coercion that accompanied two petless children. It was followed by a fish tank full of expensive tropical fish that no one but mom would feed or clean, three gerbils that all sacrificed their lives to wet tail, a tarantula named Harry S. Truman (the S stood for spider), a jar of live crickets to feed the live tarantula, and a North Carolina beach hermit crab that outgrew its shell. The private, fenced-in backyard remained dogless until we answered an ad in the newspaper for purebred Golden Retriever puppies for $150.

There are dog rescue people and dog purchasing people. Throughout my childhood, we were always dog rescue people. I remember my mom always quoting scripture: "Woe be to the man who carries the price of a dog in his pocket." (For the record, the verse is *not* found in actual Biblical scripture. The verse can only be found in the book of First Opinions written by my mother!) The fact that my mom would even pretend to make up a quote from the Bible signifies just how adamant my family was on only having rescue dogs. So the thought of purchasing a dog brought forth all kinds of familial problems. I decided we should exhaust every available kennel, and only then would we drive to New Braunfels, Texas, to see the advertised Golden Retriever puppies. Memo to self: Never take two young children who have been begging for a dog for more than a year to see a Golden Retriever puppy unless you intend on bringing said Golden Retriever puppy home.

By the time we arrived in New Braunfels, all but three of the Golden Retriever puppies were sold and on their way to their new forever homes. Left for Kimmy and Michael to covet were two males and one slightly smaller, petite female. The kids played with all three puppies in the sellers' lush green grass yard. The grass was so tall that the puppies almost disappeared into the St. Augustine carpet. Two other families drove up and quickly got out of their cars to look at the puppies while Kimmy and Michael played hide and seek.

Maybe it was the warm, soft golden fur that felt like velour against your cheek. Maybe it was the pink, hairless, protruding tummy that twitched when you rubbed it. Maybe it was the pressure knowing that others might buy our puppy before we got to. Or maybe it was the divine smell of puppy breath. But Purebred Golden Retriever puppy $150 Sunny came home with us.

A house with a dog in it is a home. Sunny gladly grew into her feet and became Kimmy's and Michael's forever friend. We survived fleas. We survived the occasional mishap of a tennis shoe that came in contact with undetected Sunny yard waste. We survived (too many to count) broken, lower-branch Christmas tree ornaments that were sacrificed by a swishing tail. We survived chewed up books, shoes, homework, sprinkler heads, and a shovel handle. We survived small holes that became two-foot trenches next to the fence where Sunny laid to keep cool. Despite the small inconveniences that came with dog ownership, when the high-pitched daily rumble of the public school bus came down the street and stopped in front of our house, Sunny would stumble over her four legs to quickly get to the door to meet her family. Knowing that Sunny was waiting there made everything perfect.

Sunny never attempted to run away. She was glad to lie in the front yard and watch her family play. Occasionally, someone would hit a tennis ball too hard, and Sunny would chase it wildly down the street, beating everyone to it. She would scoop it up in her mouth and immediately bring it back safely to her yard at her home. On walks, Sunny barely needed a leash. She was happy to walk by the side of those she adored. Once we turned the corner to make our way back to our house, Sunny would lead. She knew where home was and what was waiting for her there.

Sunny stayed with us through a litter of eight puppies. Despite my better judgment, I was convinced to allow one of Sunny's puppies to stay with us permanently. Sunny raised her pup as caring as any mother would. Then one day, size mattered. Sunny's puppy was larger than Sunny and became overly aggressive toward Michael. It would jump and push Michael to the ground and then straddle him. No longer did Michael want to play in his own back yard. As time went on, I tried to work with the pup, but its behavior was unruly. Sunny grew distant in the shadow of her pup, and her pup grew even larger and even more aggressive. No longer did Michael want to be around Sunny or any dog, for that matter.

It is heart-wrenching to see a child become afraid of an animal. My entire being was filled with sadness to see my own child become afraid of a family pet. When my parents came to visit and my father witnessed his only grandson's true fear and aversion to Sunny and her pup, my father's retired Highway Patrolman protection antenna went up. No animal was going to hurt his grandson Michael, and no grandson of his was going to grow up being afraid of a dog. My father vehemently told me that Michael was just too young to have a dog.

Leave it to parents to be parents and handle the situation. I came home from work the next day to find that my father had found two good homes for Sunny and her pup. Sunny would be going to the firehouse just around the corner from our house, and her pup would be going to a firefighter's sister's ranch where the dog could run.

Michael and Kimmy had both gone with their Papa to take the dogs to their new forever homes. At first, I was devastated and angry that my father would give away my children's dogs. Then I realized he was right. Home was where his grandchildren lived. And waiting for me at home that day was my father who loved me enough to make the tough decision, the right decision for my children and their home.

Lesson 25:

Understand The Art of Begging

Real begging only works when people trust you, like you, and want you to get the big win.

Nothing can grate on this mother's ears more than the incessant sound of a child begging for Fruit Roll Ups, Twizzlers, or Neon Sour Gummy Worms at the grocery store. With their pint-sized feet tucked in at the bottom of the grocery cart and their tiny hands in deadlock grip on the metal side of the quickly moving cart, I became one of those mothers who ignored the constant pleas for grocery items. It was always my thought that if I hurried to gather the necessary groceries and pretended the cries for certain foods were not real, the pleas would go away and I could check out and get these children home where they could whine in solitude. How, then, did I go from ignoring the begging to writing about the art of it? Well, I met Schnoodle Fay.

Fay understood the art of begging from her very first day in puppy training class. At just three months of age, Fay and our entire family enrolled in Fay's puppy classes. They were held once a week for 12 weeks on Saturday mornings. Encouraged that this was the ideal time to train our new fur addition, Robin, Kimmy, Michael, and I brought Fay to class weekly to learn lead training, potty training, basic commands like sit, stay, down, come, wait, and stop, and how to retrieve toys. More importantly, Fay would learn to socialize with other puppies.

The trainer stood at the front of the room. She was a stocky gal with blunt short-cut hair and no makeup. She was dressed in jeans and a blue golf shirt. Around her waist was a handyman's two-pocket Home Depot carpenter's apron that tied in the back. Behind her were three round makeshift playpen areas. We were instructed to place our pets in the play area that corresponded with their size.

The first round barrier was a see-through wire structure about a foot and a half high. It was for the small puppies. At less than two pounds, Fay was placed in this area along with eight or so other eager, rambunctious, barking, nipping, canine friends. Next to it was another see-through circular enclosed structure made with a wall of wire approximately three feet high. It was for medium-sized puppies. Five or so puppies occupied the second pen. The final round barrier was for larger puppies including retrievers, shepherds, Dalmatians, greyhounds, Weimaraners, and the like. The enclosure was five feet in height and had a small latch on the side so it could be opened and closed for easy access to the puppies. In it were loud, barking, rough-and-tumble puppies who were more excited to chase each other than learn.

Once all the puppies were in their appropriate places, the instructor faced us and began to lecture on puppy safety and socialization. At that precise moment, puppy Fay pushed back on her haunches and flew over her small puppy barrier, landing right next to the instructor. The audience of puppy-training parents and friends all laughed at the airborne oddity. The instructor leaned down, scooped up Fay with her right hand. With her left hand, she fumbled for a treat morsel from the front pocket of her utility apron and gently placed Fay inside the second circular pen for medium-sized puppies. As Fay safely landed on the floor of her new enclosure, the instructor gave her a small morsel and told her to "stay."

Maybe it was the laughter from the crowd, the scrumptious bite of wonderfulness supplied by the instructor, or the fact that Fay desired people more than puppy friends, but as soon as the instructor faced the crowd again and began to speak, Fay cleared the three-foot barrier and landed perfectly on the tile floor. She then scurried her way to the instructor's feet, sat perfectly, and whimpered for attention and reaction. The audience roared with laughter. This time, the instructor acknowledged her furry visitor. "Well, aren't you a little escape artist?" she said. Then she reached down once again to scoop up Fay in her right hand, retrieved another treat out of her apron pocket with her left hand, and walked to the far side of the room where the large puppy play area was located.

The puppies in the large pen were engaged in a war of fur fun, yipping, barking, tugging at each other, and plowing into the side of the playpen. Next to the large puppies, our Fay looked more like a chew toy than a potential friend. The instructor unclasped the latch and placed Fay next to the large rowdy puppies. Once again, she handed Fay a small morsel and said "stay" in a louder, firmer voice. Fay quickly ate the treat and began to beg for more. Michael was watching in horror, convinced that his Fay was soon to be devoured by the larger animals. He was adamant that the sounds from Fay were not Fay begging but Fay calling for help.

As the instructor returned to the center of the room, regained her composure, and began lecturing again, Fay's whimpers turned into much louder squeals. Michael began to shift the weight of his stance and readied himself to sprint over to the pen to recover his Fay dog from inevitable death by a large puppy. The instructor took this opportunity to caution the audience about enforcing bad behavior like Fay's begging cries and instead rewarding good behavior.

Either it was Fay seeing her boy Michael readying himself for the rescue or hearing the words of the instructor, but something made Fay move over to the side of the five-foot playpen, stretch up on her back legs, and literally climb up the enclosure like a circus dog. She hovered at the top of the pen long enough to balance herself and look directly at the audience. Then she jumped five feet down to the floor, landing with a perfect-10 dismount. Fay sprinted to the instructor and all but leaped up into her arms. The startled instructor caught Fay and cradled her in her right hand like a football close to her side and within Fay's reach of the treat apron. Fay wiggled slightly to get closer to the treats. I am pretty sure I saw her smile. It was then that we learned Fay was Houdini and also highly motivated by food. She was the ultimate beggar and honed her talent to perfection with everyone she met.

Begging got Fay in the front seat of the car on a warm, comfortable lap during long road trips. Begging got Fay in front of the air conditioner in the same car. Begging got Fay carried down the stairs so she wouldn't have to walk them. Begging got Fay placed on top of the bed, placed back down on the floor, and placed on the couch or chair. Begging got Fay freed from the kennel at the dog groomer and allowed to roam the office while others got groomed. And begging got Fay chicken purchased as one single chicken strip from the drive-through at Whataburger.

Begging to Fay became an art form. It was not the whimpering that did it. It was the combination of her head turned ever so slightly right, then left, then back to the right, along with the blinking of her long, trademark eyelashes. Fay also mastered the art of the gentle paw placed ever so slightly on your hand or leg. Finally, it was the sweet way in which she thanked you with a gentle brush of her fluffy ears against your skin, followed by a light lick of gratitude. Fay knew what she wanted and how to get it. She was relentless.

My children and I all learned from Fay's perfect begging art form. No longer did I hear the kids' incessant whining. They had put in place a refined, well executed strategy instead. When Kimmy turned 15, she got her driver's permit, and naturally, in her teenage brain, she deserved a car. Kimmy was one of the youngest kids in her class, so she came late to driving. By the time she took her first driver's ed class, many of her close friends had been driving for six months. For a solid year, we were all subjected to descriptions of auto makes and models along with a complete list of everyone she knew who received a car for their birthday or other assorted holidays.

Kimmy was cunning in her begging strategy. She would wait until a time when I was juggling her schedule, Michael's schedule, my work schedule, and our church activities as the appropriate and opportune moment to bring up a car. Just when I was trying to figure out how to get Michael's science fair poster board to the elementary school cafeteria, Kimmy to early basketball practice at her high school, and me to work on time, Kimmy would say, "If only we had another driver in our family with a safe mode of transportation that could drop off Michael and then get me to basketball practice, then pick up Michael after school and take both of us to kids' choir at church." For months, I attempted to ignore her. But I marveled at the way she always managed to throw in helping her brother out as a ploy or, better yet, play the religion card.

As her driving skills improved, I found myself often entrusting her behind the wheel of my car, but the thought and expense of actually getting another vehicle paralyzed me. Then came a scheduled, out-of-town overnight business trip that required me to hire an adult to stay with Kimmy and Michael until I returned. I tapped into my childcare network but found that the more mature and trusted choices were unavailable. That left me with a recent high school graduate, the daughter of one of my friends. This choice was a young woman barely older than Kimmy and certainly not as responsible as my own child. However, she had a car and the means to get both Kimmy and Michael to their schools and activities and to the emergency room if need be. The going rate for overnight childcare and school drop-off/pick-up services was $100 a day. I wrote out the check for $400 and realized that with just one business trip a month, I could afford a car for Kimmy.

I began the search for a clean, safe, well maintained used car, but I kept it totally secret from Kimmy. She continued with her car-begging strategy. At times, her manipulation and purposeful use of words made me smile to myself. She had become a pro at begging. On the phone, I heard her making plans for an after-school event, and then she turned away from the phone and shouted at me, "Mom, I know it is *really* (melodramatic stress to the word *really*) inconvenient you having to drive me all the way to Lindsay's and then *interrupt* (emphatic emphasis added to the word *interrupt*) your day to drive all the way back over and pick me up tomorrow. But can I spend the night at Lindsay's, or would it be easier for you and Mikey (perfect use of her brother as a pawn) if Lindsay drove herself here and stayed at our house?" Again, I ignored her begging, but somehow, I did appreciate the fact that Kimmy had honed that art.

There were several more verbal innuendos, well placed turns of a phrase, and strategic manipulations. In the end, Kimmy did get a car, and I got another driver in the house who could run errands for me.

The art of begging is a learned trait. Fay learned it. Kimmy learned it. Begging lands somewhere between manipulation and honing in on your relationship to make a person actually feel rather sorry for you. I have never really taught sales teams how to beg, but often when revenue was too close to making actual budget, I demonstrated how a well-placed sales call, coupled with the art of begging, shored up the month and guaranteed budget.

Real begging only works when people trust you. They must also like you and want you to get the win. Constant begging is always annoying. Picture the sales associate at a furniture store who constantly interrupts you and says, "Can I help you, please?" "What can I help you with?" "Can I show something else?" To me, it sounds like "I work on commission, and I'd love for you to buy something from me today."

The art of begging is the difference between Schnoodle Fay—daintily touching your hand with her paw, cocking her head ever so slightly to the left and right, batting her long eyelashes at you in order to get a bite of your chicken—and an aggressive mongrel almost taking off your fingers. Better to learn the art of begging than to bite the hand that feeds you.

Lesson 26:

Never Forget There's A Puppy In All Of Us

Life is too serious to be taken all that seriously.

The smell of puppy breath should be bottled and sold. I am sure it would become the next Bond fragrance and take the market by storm. Puppy breath is oh so sweet smelling and usually follows that deep-stretching, full-body yawn that comes after a puppy has wrestled, tumbled, rolled, and tousled in unconditional play. Often it comes with sweet, gentle, puppy-sized licks. Puppy breath and the puppies that produce it are a joy to my heart.

And then there's puppy love—that adoring, worshipful affection. It is the soft velveteen coat, the round pink belly, the small almost inaudible whimpers, and the antics. The uncontrollable desire to play, explore, and discover. The ability to find pleasure and newness in everything. With puppy love, no one is ever a stranger, no obstacle is too insurmountable to tackle, and no item should not be tasted and chewed. And after a long day of uncontrollable frolic and fun, puppies sleep soundly and peacefully. If only puppies could stay puppies forever!

Why can't they?

Brandy appeared one day in the front yard of my child-hood home in Phoenix. My father said she must have been yet another victim—an abandoned dog dropped off in the Arizona desert to fend for itself or die. Her brown-and-white coat was matted near her tail. Her darker, almost black face was desert sand dusty. Her eyes were caked near the corners with dirt and dried tears. Around her drooling mouth were wads of dirt and slobber, but she was happy to see us. Standing tall on all fours, her head met my dad's hips. Her flinging tail hit with such force that it threw even my almost six-foot father off balance. Brandy weighed more than 140 pounds. "Let her drink water," Dad told my three sisters and me, forcing us to wait before we all lunged toward her to shower her with little girl hugs and pats to her large body. Brandy was a full-grown St. Bernard.

Once Brandy was hydrated, we descended on her, lavishing her dirty coat with our affections. Her enormous body quiv-ered with excitement. Occasionally, she turned her head back toward the eight hands that busily stroked her, just long enough to repay our kindness with kisses. Her large, slobbery tongue covered our entire arms, leaving them completely drenched in dog spit. "Give her some room," Dad commanded, "and let's get her something to eat."

At that time, our home was filled with four Chihuahuas: Pancho, Blanco, Gomer Pyle, and Archie Bunker. Dad brought out the small five-pound sack of bite-sized dog kibble and began placing food in front of Brandy, one small scoop at a time. As Dad dropped the food into the plastic makeshift feeding bowl, Brandy inhaled it like a vacuum, not leaving even one small nugget. Dad filled that bowl more than a dozen times. Brandy was not just a St Bernard; she seemed to be part horse.

The remainder of the day was filled with a bath. Due to

her immense size, the bath had to take place in the backyard. Dad attached the garden hose to the water heater inside the laundry room and ran the hose out the laundry room window to the backyard patio. One of my sisters ran in the house and grabbed the Flex shampoo from our bathtub. I remember handfuls of shampoo suds floating in the air and falling to the ground like snow. It seemed like hours of scrubbing, rinsing, scrubbing, and rinsing, with Brandy shaking off the excess shampoo, water, or both between each shampooing. The warm water and the eight little girl hands running down every inch of Brandy must have delighted her since she remained standing in the same spot the entire time. She even allowed us to wash near her eyes, tail, feet, and ears. During this much-needed beauty day, Brandy never growled once or made a sound.

Brandy was clean, and her fur smelled like one of us girls. She was happy. Then came the drying. Brandy again leaned into our hands, relinquishing all control to us, just like a playful puppy does with its mother. Brandy was indeed full-grown, but what a puppy she still was! Despite her girth, she allowed my sisters and me to lead her, dress her up, sleep on her, and even harness her to pull us down the street on our skateboards and bikes. All 140-plus pounds of her were sheer pleasure for us. Two parents, one grandmother, four girls, four Chihuahuas, and one full-grown St. Bernard make living in an 1,800-square-foot home a bit cramped. But we considered it cozy.

One day, Brandy's puppy-like antics made her dart in front of my Grandma Bailey, causing her to turn quickly to avoid a fall. As Grandma turned, her leg bumped the corner of a coffee table near a chair. The quick incident peeled back her paper-thin skin on her leg, leaving a massive bleeding wound. Dad decided that Brandy needed more space to play. Brandy was taken to my father's auction lot and immediately became a watchdog.

Playful, full-grown dogs that have never outgrown their puppyhood do not make good watchdogs. Over the course of the next few months, Brandy became the brunt of an illegal prank. Down the street from my father's auction lot was a rather rustic bar. Patrons of the bar leaned more toward rugged bikers than sophisticated connoisseurs. One night before closing, two of the patrons who had been drinking heavily got into a disagreement about how much the St. Bernard in the auction lot down the street must weigh. Disagreement turned into a bet. The bet turned into a dare. And the dare turned into a six-foot hole being cut into the chain link fence at Dad's auction lot and playful, puppy-like Brandy being led down to the bar to be hoisted up on a scale and weighed. The next morning, the police recovered Brandy from behind the bar. Tied up to the gas meter pole was lovable Brandy, tail wagging with helicopter force, lavishing kisses on anyone who came near her, and oh so ready to be fed breakfast.

Nothing Dad did could make Brandy relinquish her inner puppy qualities and become more watchdog fierce. She was a gregarious, full-grown puppy, and now more than 150 pounds. Brandy was moved to the inner auction lot where she was less likely to be stolen again. Then Brandy did the unimaginable. Early one morning, Dad went down to the auction lot to feed Brandy and the other dogs. Brandy, forgetting the magnitude of her size, stature, and strength, and undoubtedly eager to be fed, met Dad with all her inner puppyish might. She leaped up on her hind legs to greet Dad and literally knocked over my nearly six-foot, hefty-built, ex-highway patrolman father, causing him to fall and break three ribs. As he lay on the ground in pain, Brandy slathered Dad with kisses. The auction lot was no place for this gentle giant. Dad slowly recovered, and Brandy was given to dear friends who had a beautiful farm in Camp Verde, Arizona. Brandy lived out her full-grown years as the best puppy they ever had.

Her name was Lisa. She was kind of a Brandy in human form. I actually never hired her, but she was hired on the spot by my boss while he was trying on shoes during lunch. In less than a quarter of an hour, she had managed to convince him to buy three pairs of Ferragamo shoes at full price. He returned to the CBS television station, which he managed, and told me I had a new account executive starting in two weeks. Lisa had no media experience. No history in television. No real connection to Central New York, let alone Syracuse. And she would become a legacy.

Lisa was 23 years old at the time. I was just past 30. A native of Boston, Lisa had a rough nasalness to her voice and consistently dropped her r's when she spoke. She was attractive, muscular. She had a gymnast's body as exemplified by her muscular thighs and calves, and at a moment's notice, she would demonstrate her gymnastic prowess with front flips and half pikes down the hallway. Her dark brown hair cascaded down to her shoulders in coils of curls that bounced as she walked. Actually, she was just plain bouncy and effervescently bubbly and thus very likable. She entered a room with childlike glee and playful curiosity. She was joyful and winsome. She was so like Brandy. And I adored her.

There was no training Lisa. She just naturally sold. Every day was a new adventure. Every sales call was an opportunity to learn, explore, and play. Just when life got serious, Lisa would turn to you, stick out her tongue, move it quickly back and forth from side to side and then exclaim, "Look, I swallowed a puppy!" Secretly, she was my favorite account executive. Secretly, she was everyone's favorite.

Lisa was married to Greg, a young man who had been born into a family of doctors. His father was a surgeon, and he, too, was destined to become the next renowned medical professional. But something happened to him. Lisa happened. Suddenly, Greg was no longer on his medical school trajectory. Instead, he became a roadie for the rock band Guns N' Roses. Daily, Lisa entertained us with stories and pictures of her playful life.

Over the course of her tenure, Lisa became more like my adopted daughter than an employee. Greg traveled all the time, and my husband Ed worked the 6:00 p.m. and 11:00 p.m. newscast in an adjacent market with an hour commute each way. With no family to go home to, Lisa and I spent time in the office dreaming dreams, creating proposals, and coming up with sales ideas long after others had gone home for the day. It was during these late evenings that I discovered Lisa had a young-at-heart spirit inside her that would not allow her to ever grow up. She was lightning in a bottle and, like a soft, warm cuddly puppy, brought out the best in people. Nothing was impossible for Lisa.

One weekend, Lisa's client scheduled a showcase of homes event, and Lisa asked me to accompany her. Gladly relishing an opportunity to tour fancy, new homes, I agreed. Unbeknownst to Lisa, Greg had gotten a weekend off and was coming home to surprise her. Greg came to the showcase of homes with Lisa. When I got there, Lisa was beaming to have her husband next to her at one of her client's events.

Then the day wore on, and Greg wore out. I remember sitting on a bench outside, directly in front of the best-in-show home. Greg was sitting next to me. He looked pale and exhausted. I looked at him and asked if he felt alright. Greg shook his head no and said his hand really hurt. He had gotten a $3\frac{1}{2}$-inch splinter in his hand as he was building the scaffolding for the lighting rig for the next Guns N' Roses concert.

He had had the splinter removed by one of the other roadies, had poured some soap and water on it, and wrapped it up in a bandage. My maternal side kicked in, and I reached for his hand to inspect the situation. As I did, I felt the heat coming out of his fingers. I then touched his forehead. It was on fire. "Lisa," I said, "Greg needs to get to a doctor. Now!"

The next hours were a whirlwind for Lisa. Greg's hand had gotten infected, and as infections do, it had manifested itself in the weakest part of Greg's body—his heart valve. Greg was 24 years old. Within a day, he was being prepped for a heart valve replacement. His parents flew in, specialists were called, prayers were said. I remember sitting with Lisa and talking about the situation. There sat my young friend, my unsinkable employee who was trying to figure out how she could preserve Greg's manhood in case he died.

"I just need to convince Greg to freeze his sperm before he has surgery," Lisa told me, "so I can have his child later on." Her comment was pure never-grow-up Lisa in all its purity.

Greg survived surgery, recovered fully, and Lisa eventually got pregnant. Shortly after she had their first child, she relocated back to Boston and took a job with a major telecom.

For years, Lisa's stories filled the hallways of our station. She was a ray of sunshine, undeniably contagious, and always allowing her childlike zest for life to penetrate the very walls of the building. Her clients were sad to see her go. Not only did they miss her fun-loving spirit, but to many, she had become like a member of their own family.

Lisa and I kept in touch for a few years. There were annual holiday greeting cards, birthday cards, and the occasional phone call. Then, distance and busy lives made us lose each other. One day years later, I took to social media to find Lisa. A thorough search turned up Greg but no Lisa. How sad, I thought. Greg and Lisa must have divorced.

Months later, I received a Facebook message from Greg. It

was long and filled with words of anguish, deep pain, and dark sadness. Lisa had died years earlier of brain cancer. Greg had been left with their beautiful children and the memory of Lisa's uncontainable, unstoppable joy. I read Greg's message over again and again while drowning in my should-have, could-have thoughts. Questions of regret flooded my mind. Of anyone in all the world, why take Lisa?

Lisa had given me permission to be young at heart, always adventurous and joy-germ happy. She made me believe that no one ever was a stranger and no obstacle was too insurmountable to tackle. I learned that life should be an uncontrollable frolic and fun.

Throughout my career, I have told new hires that we need to both have fun and make money. If we only make money and have no fun, we will not want to keep our job. If we have fun but don't make money, we won't keep our jobs. And, short of doing something illegal or immoral, I can't imagine having more fun and making more money than I have in the media and advertising industry.

Life is too serious to be taken all that seriously. Today, when I stick out my tongue, move it quickly back and forth from side to side, I am reminded that there is a puppy, a Brandy, even a Lisa in all of us.

Lesson 27:

Don't Be Afraid To Make A Little Noise

Noise creates change. Change creates a more productive environment.

Schnoodle Sam is our Bob Barker. Despite his limited stature, his voice is mighty. He warns of the UPS or FedEx delivery person who haphazardly intrudes on his front porch and uninvitingly drops packages at his front door. He calls our attention every other week to the four lawn men who unload their mowers and edgers in our front yard. And he barks at the red tin can marked "treats" that strategically sits on top of the tall mirrored dresser in our bedroom, commanding it to open itself or, better yet, plunge to the floor for easier canine access.

Sam is not a quiet dog except when he is eating or sleeping; however, his calls of the wild are not unprovoked or unwarranted. Sam makes noises to get my attention, and I know that when he barks, there is always reasoning and justification behind it.

I have never been a whistleblower, although I am one of the first people to stand up for my children, my people, and my clients. I will defend any underdog and right all injustices using my loud and clear voice of experience, learned wisdom, and fortitude. I have all but screamed to get policies changed, individuals promoted, or rules rewritten. But my greatest reward has come from teaching others to use their "bark" to make changes, make something known, or just make others take note.

Lynne was a nymph of a woman—five feet three inches tall at best and skeletally thin. Her ultra-fine, thinning blonde hair coupled with her gaunt physique and pencil-thin limbs made her look a lot like a drowned rat. She spoke in low, hushed tones but was superb at her job. Lynne was hired in our television station's traffic department to input commercial schedule orders.

The traffic department operated as the brains and continuity of the sales department. A salesperson would sell a client a marketing schedule that included a set number of commercials. Then the traffic department made sure the client's commercials were scheduled and aired with the correct piece of commercial copy on the correct days in the correct programs they had desired. Lynne was a savant at data entry, paid great attention to detail, and did her job exceptionally well. Lynne was irreplaceable, which is why it was such an inconvenience when Lynne was out of the office for personal reasons or illness.

At work, calling in sick required an actual phone call to a supervisor. In Lynne's case, it was the traffic manager, who reported to me. Many mornings I came into the office to find that Lynne had called in sick. Lynne's absence made for a less-than-easy day, and many times, when Lynne returned, she had a sprained wrist, an abrasion on her arm, or a limp to her walk. Most people thought that Lynne's frailness resulted in lots of falls or that Lynne was just a klutz. Two days off here, a day off there. The days off added up until Lynne was quickly running out of paid time off. When she came back to work one time, I called her into my office to address the time off issue. My main thought was, "What can I do to help?" Lynne looked down into her lap as we spoke. Her eyes appeared to be closed, and her tiny hands were folded in front of her. Lynne nodded a few times but said nothing.

Weeks later, Lynne called in sick again. When she returned from her two days off, she had a broken nose. Beneath her eyes were raccoon-like bands of black and blue. Her nose was fat and swollen twice its size. It looked like it belonged on someone else's face, not hers. It was taped with white surgical tape. When I saw her, I took her hand and walked her into my office.

"What happened?" I asked softly. Tears filled her eyes, and her mouth became dry like it was filled with cotton.

"How can I help?" I said. I watched the line of tears begin to stream down her cheeks. They pooled up on the white tape across her nose, and once enough tears had accumulated, they flowed down quickly to her chin, peppering her dark hooded top with spots and streaks.

"Who did this?" I whispered close to her ear. She looked down and quickly said her husband's name in a hushed, low, but audible tone. Lynne had conjured up enough of her inner fire to make some noise and get my attention. I reached over and softly held her until her tears ended. Then I took her hand and asked her if she was ready to do something about it. She nodded yes. Slowly, I helped her stand, and we walked down to the office of my boss, the general manager. Usually verbose and gregarious, he immediately sensed the struggle and came forward to take hold of Lynne's other arm.

Lynne stayed in his office through the police interviews and HR conversations. By the end of the day, arrangements had been made for someone to retrieve Lynne's personal things from her home. Lynne now had a safe place to stay indefinitely, and we had found a way to tap into a station client to handle all the legal paperwork and ultimate divorce.

Over the next few months, a metamorphosis took place. Lynne grew in courage and confidence. She held her head high, and her smile came back. When my traffic manager announced her retirement, Lynne was quickly promoted to that leadership position. Lynne, still only five feet three inches tall, grew taller every day in inner strength. Before I left the station, she had become a well-equipped, respected manager capable of voicing her ideas for change, processes, and people. She had gained pride and self-respect. No longer was her tiny voice afraid to make some noise.

Too often in my past, I have seen good people leave good companies or strong relationships simply because they were fearful of making a little noise and getting a little attention. They hid behind the shadows, afraid to voice their concerns, desires, wants, and needs. Once the situation got unbearable, they frequently shut down, stopped being productive, or even left the company. I have found that providing a safe environment where words are not used as weapons, opinions at all levels hold weight, and management pride is not allowed to get in the way, people feel free to make a little noise.

Christina was one of those potential noisemakers. She was an executive assistant to the owner of a mid-sized financial firm which was one of Robin and my business clients. She was a smart, strong-willed, incredibly attractive woman who had been moved around the globe with her military husband. When I met her, she had two small children and was working on her master's degree.

Christina watched and listened intently as Robin and I proposed change management strategies that would help take the financial firm on an upward trajectory. She was eager to help us implement systems and processes. She asked intelligent questions and had great ideas for the growth of the organization.

Once during a one-on-one session with Christina, I asked where she saw herself fitting into the newly structured organization. Christina looked at me and said, "I want to be the president of our firm." "Then do it," I said. "Wear the suit, put on your big girl shoes, and let the CEO know that is what you want." My words seemed to give Christina the fuel she needed to use her voice. Within six years, she was CEO of the firm and even made the list of San Antonio's Forty Under-Forty Leaders to watch.

Noise creates change. Change creates a more productive environment. When things get too quiet at home or in the office, something is undoubtedly wrong. My father always said that the squeaky wheel got the grease. He was right. Making noise gets someone's attention.

In the case of Schnoodle Sam, a well-placed outburst usually got someone to open the red tin treat can for him.

Lesson 28:

Listen Intently

I like to listen. I have learned a great deal from listening carefully. Most people never listen.

—*Ernest Hemingway*

When we lived in Cazenovia, our German Shepherd Greta had a very keen sense of hearing. When she slept out on the deck, which overlooked the yard below, the breaking of a simple twig down by the stream a half acre away could wake her up. She heard tiny shrews playing in the central vacuum wall plug long before we knew what a shrew even was. When you spoke to her, her ears tilted up and inward, and she turned her head and looked directly at your lips.

After Greta had settled into her home with us, she kept me company at night when my husband Ed was working. I treasured our long walks around the north end of Cazenovia Lake after dinner. But when Greta heard anything that remotely resembled a deer or squirrel nearby, she lunged at her leash, all but jerking my shoulder out of its socket.

Then I found out I was pregnant with Kimmy. Hearing parenting words of my father echoing in my head, I knew it was time for Greta to get her dog manners in check and get formally trained. An ad in the local neighborhood throwaway newspaper revealed the name of a private dog trainer in Canastota, New York, not too far from where we lived.

Our first lesson was on Saturday. If you have never been through professional dog training, let me forewarn you. The pet owners, not the dogs, get most of the training. I have found that dogs are naturally smart, but we humans need to learn how to walk our animals, talk to our animals, and lead our animals.

The morning was hot and sunny. Greta behaved perfectly with the trainer. With Greta's thin, short leather lead attached to a choke chain, the trainer placed Greta by her left hip. The leather lead, held loosely in her left hand, crossed over the trainer's body. That left the trainer's right hand free to give signals. As the trainer weaved in and out of stakes placed in the ground, Greta walked perfectly next to her, weaving in and out in harmony and sequence. When the trainer stopped, Greta stopped, and with a slight upward tug on the leash, Greta's head was lifted slightly, signaling her to sit tall and prideful at the trainer's side. Greta worked hard with the trainer and then with both Ed and me. As a reward for all the hard work, Greta was given an ice cube, which she loved.

The trainer spent hours teaching us the basics, but the real training was in teaching Greta to obey hand signals. I remember thinking at the time how odd it was that we were having Greta, a dog who had supernatural hearing powers, learn to obey hand signals. The trainer assured me that even dogs with exceptional hearing need to be so focused on you as their lead that they watch your body and react to your visual cues and signals.

So it was that Greta learned that when I placed my hand

palm down and moved it toward my hip, she would lie down. When I held my hand up, palm facing outward, she would stop. Motion my hand to come toward me, Greta would immediately come, and if I curved my palm toward my body and move it up slightly like I was scooping up water, Greta would sit. Greta also mastered speak and no bark/no fuss with simple hand movements. She became the best example of a well-behaved dog.

Raising a German Shepherd while living out in the country created a few health challenges for Greta. Ticks were rampant, so we had the yard sprayed often. The heat, humidity, and rain made Greta susceptible to ear mites and yeast infections in her ears. Although we were fastidious about keeping Greta clean, she scratched her ears and shook her head constantly to ease the itchiness deep inside her head.

A few summers after Kimmy was born, we took Greta to a new vet who had been recommended by friends at work. The vet had graduated from Cornell, one of the most prestigious veterinary schools in the country and had taught for many years there. The visit was routine annual shots; however, the vet suggested that we bring Greta back to be anesthetized so he could perform a thorough cleaning of her ears and see if we could get her ear infections under control. We made another appointment and dropped off Greta a week later for her special ear cleaning.

When it was time to pick up Greta, I put Kimmy in her car seat in the back seat and drove to Syracuse. It was raining when we left, so I had put Kimmy's pink hoodie up over her head. When we arrived, I unbuckled Kimmy and carried her into the vet's office. The office staff led Greta out on a leash. When Kimmy saw her, she immediately reached out her hands and called Greta's name, but Greta didn't turn toward her. Maybe it was the pink hoodie that looked unfamiliar to Greta, but once Greta recognized me, her tail began to wag. I paid the bill, led Greta outside into the rain, and secured both Greta and Kimmy into the back seat. Greta seemed sleepy the entire way home. Her head rested on the edge of Kimmy's car seat.

When we got home about 45 minutes later, both Greta and Kimmy were sound asleep. I pulled into the driveway, got out of the car, and opened the back door. The sound of the door opening did not disturb either of the sleeping girls. But once the cool air from outside flowed into the car and hit Greta's face, she woke up and jumped out of the car. My parents were visiting from Arizona, and my father met me in the garage and took sleeping Kimmy in his arms. Greta followed him into the house. Her tail was sunken down between her legs. She walked slowly and cautiously into the house. For the rest of the evening, Greta was mopey and not her happy dog self. Later that night, Ed came home from work. When he came into the bedroom to get undressed, Greta was sound asleep on the floor next to my side of the bed. She did not get up to greet him.

The following morning, Greta bounced into the kitchen where my father was making coffee. The sound of the coffee grinder didn't seem to faze her. While I headed back to the bathroom to get ready for work, Dad went outside to get the paper, and Greta followed behind him. Once out in the front yard, Greta saw a squirrel and took off running. My dad called for her, but she did not respond to his call. He came back in to get me, but by the time I headed toward the front yard, Greta had made her way back to the house and ran inside the door. My father shook his head and made some sort of sarcastic comment under his breath.

It was a normal busy workday for me. I returned home at my usual time, exhausted but just in time for dinner. The kitchen smelled wonderful. There was nothing better than having my parents visit. Kimmy was playing on the floor in the kitchen. Greta was sleeping next to one of the kitchen chairs. Dad had the volume up loud on the TV in the kitchen. Mom, carrying plates of food to the table, nudged at Greta with her foot and told her to move. The touch of Mom's shoe startled Greta from her nap, and she quickly relocated herself to the other end of the kitchen. It was then that Dad said the unimaginable. "Sandy, I don't think this dog can hear anymore." Suddenly, dinner didn't matter. I called for Greta to come, but she did not come. I walked over toward her, faced her, and begin to give her verbal commands. "Sit." "Shake." Greta did nothing. I ran into the living room to find one of Greta's squeaky toys and squeaked it the entire way back into the kitchen. It wasn't until Greta saw the toy in my hand that she reacted with her puppy-like excitement. Dad was right. I called the vet and left a frantic message with the answering service.

The next day, I heard from the vet. They assured me that it was simply the after-effects of the deep ear cleaning. They were wrong. Greta was totally, incurably deaf. Something had happened, and no one wanted to take responsibility.

For the remainder of her life, Greta learned to listen with her eyes and with her entire body. She listened with her fur to the vibrations of footsteps around her. She listened to my hands intently as she was led on a leash. Hand signals became our voice to her. She learned to listen and respond to the porch lights flashing on and off to signal her to come in from the dark yard at night. Her sense of smell grew even stronger. Often, she would lift her nose up to the air as if to "listen" for the scents of food, rain, Kimmy, or danger. I watched Greta learn to survive in her new, silent world. Greta taught me how to listen.

There are not a lot of good books written on listening. But learning to listen intently is one of the single most important attributes anyone can have. Too often, we listen to what is being said with the intent to answer, comment, or respond. Instead, we should listen with the intent to understand. I think of new, inexperienced sellers who are so set on sharing their knowledge or the details of their products or services with the potential client that they never listen to the potential client outlining exactly what their needs are. Worse yet, the eager-to-impress salespeople literally keep on talking through the customer's yes and end up with a no.

When I was in high school, I took notes on classroom lectures and meetings in spiral notebooks. In college, I sold copies of my class notes to failing students and made a small business out of it. I still write everything (phone calls, meetings, sales calls, lectures, training sessions) in spiral notebooks, time coding and date stamping them. My notes signaled to clients and others that what they said was important enough for me to write down. It also gave me a chance to parrot back what I heard. Many a successful outcome has been created simply because I had the ability to recall precisely what was desired and when it was articulated.

I have also learned to listen with my eyes. I carefully study the surroundings of an office or room. I watch and study body language, the physical reaction to the words that are being presented, and then use these details, together with the connotation and denotation of each word said, to form my assumptions. Listening intently is a learned skill. I think about all the business that has been lost by companies when someone uttered the phrase, "They just didn't listen to me."

I fear for this new world of business associates and our children with all their technological advances. Somewhere in all the texting and emojis, people are forgetting how important it is to just talk to each other and really listen to what people are actually saying. Words are so powerful, and the spoken word still has the ability to inspire, calm, provoke, teach, warn, and soothe.

Greta lost her ability to hear. But maybe the lesson in her loss was that she did not lose her ability to listen—to really listen.

Lesson 29:

You Are Indeed A Purebred

People who are told they are significant believe that they are significant—if they are told it enough times.

"Free to a good home" is how my sister described Paprika. Picture the *Because of Winn-Dixie* dog (a Picardy Shepherd with shaggy eyebrows, full French-looking beard and mustache, and erect ears that literally have old man hair coming out of them). Now put that canine face on a full-sized Dachshund who is height-challenged with a stocky body. Invert the front paws so they are slightly bow-legged, add in a *Star Wars* Chewbacca-like howl, and you have Paprika, my dog niece.

Paprika was adopted 10 plus years or so ago by my oldest sister Dawn and her husband Mike and has been immortalized on every holiday photo card my sister has ever sent. In my personal card collection, I have pictures of Paprika with bunny ears, Paprika holding Cupid's arrows, donning Santa's hats and reindeer antlers, riding witches' brooms, holding pumpkins, coming out of pots of gold, blowing out birthday candles, and

185

wearing sombreros. Paprika is so unusual looking that her like-ness seems perfectly natural on greeting cards. Paprika is a mutt, a mixed-breed, a Heinz 57 variety, free-to-a-good-home canine.

In her own eyes, Paprika is a purebred. Never have I seen a dog hold its head more proudly. Paprika does not know that her over-sized head doesn't quite fit her body. Nor does she know that the hair coming out of her ears looks foreign. Just call her name, and she maneuvers on her short legs toward you, collides her large head against whatever body part you have closest to her, and actually smiles. Say the word *Frisbee*, and she howls in her Chewbacca voice until you throw it across her desert yard so she can waddle after it and find it. Nowhere in her head does Paprika know she borders on absurd looking. She is confident and beautiful. She knows she is—because my sister Dawn shows her daily that she is.

When we bought Schnoodle Fay, we were exposed to the drama and confusion that existed between the American Kennel Club and the Continental Kennel Club. Fay's lineage was from a mother who was a champion American Kennel Club miniature Poodle and a father who was a champion American Kennel Club miniature Schnauzer. (We found out right away that in order to make a Schnoodle, you need both a Schnauzer and a Poodle. Schnoodles cannot make Schnoo-dles.) However, in all the lineage upheaval, we were told that Fay should be registered since she was a purebred dog. However, she could only be registered with the Continental Kennel Club because the American Kennel Club did not recognize the Schnoodle breed. If that were not confusing enough, we were asked to sign papers stating that we would not breed Fay because Schnoodles cannot have Schnoodle puppies. Purebred or not, Fay was, to us, our special dog. Fay knew she was special because we showed her daily that she was special.

Throughout my 30-plus years in media and consulting, I have dealt with an abundance of personality types, skill levels, ranges of experience, and ages. But regardless, few of these personality types who worked with me, for me, or ultimately against me genuinely believed they were purebred masters of their craft.

Daily, it seemed, much of my work effort was spent talking people off their proverbial ledges and, once they were on somewhat stable ground, filling their minds and egos with motivational pep talks to fuel them back up again. How is it that these successful professionals functioned daily without believing they were, in fact, special and had allowed themselves to get to a point where they needed constant affirmation in order to succeed at their jobs?

I believe there is a direct correlation between being significant and being successful. But over time, the order of the two has somehow gotten reversed. Instead of significant people becoming successful, today so much hinges on being successful first and then, maybe, if the moon and stars align, considering yourself significant.

When I began in the media business, I began my career selling for a small, unlistened-to AM radio station. I took home $116.72 every two weeks as a draw against future sales commissions. Despite my less-than-poverty wages, I entered into my career at the age of 21 knowing that I was significant. I was raised by loving parents in what I perceived was a normal family environment. I had three sisters, and we shared everything from bedrooms to a single bathroom with my mom (so my dad could have his boy's bathroom all to himself). We were expected to help with the cooking, the laundry, the cleaning, and the yard work, simply because my parents said we ate it, we wore it, we made it dirty, and we played in that yard.

I attended a large public school in Phoenix, Arizona, where it was part of the required curriculum to participate in everything from sports to music and art, regardless of your skill level, in order to learn to appreciate the fundamentals of sports and music and art. If I excelled at a particular sport, I made the school intramural, junior varsity, or varsity teams. If I did not excel, I was not selected for the team. The best artwork from the entire school won awards. If you were not very artistic, your artwork was not chosen to hang in the cafeteria or administration hallway. Instead, you got the choice of either bringing it home or throwing it away. If you worked hard, mastered the material, and studied, you got good grades. I never remember my parents having to call the teacher to barter, threaten, cajole, or try to defend my inferior work. I never remember my parents even knowing who most of my teachers were.

At night, we gathered as a family and ate dinner together. Then, depending on whose day it was, you did the dishes. Next was homework, and then you played outside or got to watch whatever your parents were watching on the television. I grew up feeling I was significant because my parents, teachers, sisters, friends, neighbors, and relatives all showed me I was significant. My success as a professional, leader, wife, and mother came out of knowing I was already significant before I even took on the roles of professional, leader, wife, or mother.

Today, with the significant-success order reversing, it is often unachievable because "success" is individualistic and measured differently by each of us. Then, when a person's definition of success does not come with any type of immediacy, off to the proverbial ledge many go to sit and stare unproductively or even sometimes threatening to jump. This process requires already time-constrained managers (or mothers) and supervisors (or spouses) to step back from managing and supervising in order to become cheerleaders, counselors, motivational speakers, and coaches.

After 30 years of managing for some great (and not so great) companies, being in some great (and not so great) relationships, and raising some great (but not always *perfectly* great) kids into adulthood, it occurred to me that it would be so much easier if we just started each day with a little more cheerleading, counseling, motivational pep talking, and coaching in the bathroom mirror first thing each morning and then later on to everyone we meet along our daily path, thus making all those around us feel a little bit more significant.

In my journey as a leader, I have witnessed firsthand that people who are shown they are significant (and shown it enough times) believe they are significant. It is as simple as teaching any dog a new trick. If you want a dog to sit, you can either gently push the dog's behind down and say "sit" and then reward the dog with praise for achieving the correct response, or you can put a delectable treat like a little peanut butter on the back of a wooden spoon, hold it up in front of the dog just out of reach, and then move the spoon up and back toward the dog's nose until it naturally sits. Once sitting is achieved, say "sit" and allow the dog to taste the rewards of his good efforts.

Dogs *and people* who are shown they are significant enough times believe they are significant. The point is that significant people breed a whole lot more success than successful people do who are still trying to figure out how to be significant.

I have never struggled with demonstrating to someone that they were, indeed, a purebred. And the results of my efforts were almost always rewarded by their success. My ability to effervescently lift up the down-and-outers came as natural to me as the wag of a dog's tail is to a dog. The recipe for breeding significance is easy: Simply acknowledge where a person is in their daily struggle and offer your time and attention, along with basic kindness and respect. Solving their problem does not necessarily create their significance. Allowing them to talk through their plight and solve their own problems does. Pets and people need to feel like they matter, like they have a purpose, and like their purpose contributes to a greater good. That knowledge breeds significance.

I am sure that Schnoodle Sam does not know he is not a Great Dane when he pushes his head between two spindles on the staircase upstairs and barks uncontrollably at the person delivering the mail in front of his house. Sam is doing his job to protect our home from being attacked by junk mail or death by periodicals. Sam knows that this small job is important to us.

When Paprika uses her Chewbacca-like howl to signal that the Frisbee is flying through the air, it is her way of telling my sister Dawn that she will rescue her from the flying object, attempt to capture it mid-air, and then shake it senselessly in her jaws until it can fly no more. Paprika is doing her job to eradicate the world from Frisbee overpopulation. Paprika knows that this activity not only pleases my sister Dawn but that this small Frisbee eradication is important to her.

Dogs get their significance from the happiness they bring to their people. Being purebred is not about size, lineage, or the color of our coats. Being purebred is a state of mind. Thank goodness we all have the ability to know we are, indeed, a purebred.

Lesson 30:

Take Time To Smell the Flowers

I like it better here where I can just sit quietly and smell the flowers.

—*Ferdinand the Bull (Munro Leaf)*

There is a wonderful children's book written in 1936 by Munro Leaf called *The Story of Ferdinand*. It is about a bull named Ferdinand who, unlike the other bulls who prefer to fight, loves to just sit and smell the flowers. There is a Ferdinand in every dog I have ever owned. Schnoodle Sam is no exception. However, it is not just flowers that Sam loves to smell. It is everything.

Signal to Sam that you are going to go out and get in the car, and he all but quivers. For Sam, the car means rolled down windows, and rolled-down windows mean air, and air means an olfactory overload of street smells. With the window only a fraction of the way down for safety, Sam is best situated in the front seat lap of a passenger. If he maneuvers his back paws just right, he can dig into the passenger's thighs with such force that he can sturdy his stance enough to balance his front paws on the frame of the passenger door. Then, if he bends forward, he can wedge his snout out the slightly cracked window and allow the wind that aerodynamically peels its way back against the side of the car, to hit his Schnoodle beard full force. There, at that precise blend of balance and wind-whipped beard, Sam can take in the potpourri symphony of sensations.

I have often imagined it to be as close to euphoria as any dog can get. Sam is caught between being hypnotized by the smells of the wind and his struggle to balance on his hind legs at a 45-degree angle. That forces the passenger to hold Sam tighter and shuffle their thighs a bit so as not to get bruised by the constant pressure of Sam's forceful four-inch legs digging in for stability. Then comes the inevitable clearing of the nostrils. The quick hiss of moist air pushed out of Sam's nose is somewhere between a sneeze and a large puff. Sam licks off the droplets of moisture that have built up on his nose and readies himself for another round of deep sniffing action. Once filled with what must be thousands of grand smells, Sam pulls his head back in the car. His beard is now flattened on both sides of his face, and his eyebrows are smushed back against his forehead.

I have often wondered what drug-like sensation that wind in a dog's face creates. When not in the car, his nose is held up high. Sam has a great sniffing nose. Maybe Sam would have been better suited for seeking out truffles or perhaps drugs, but instead, our Sam is content to bask in the simple house smells and the occasional rolled-down-window car ride.

In 13½ years, I have discovered that Sam hates the smell of all types of perfumes and colognes but loves the smell of bacon or anything dead in the yard. This dog of mine cannot wait to feel the wind from a car ride but detests the ceiling fan above him blowing air in his face. He likes the smell of fresh water poured from the Brita pitcher but would probably rather drink out of an unflushed toilet if he could reach it. He can sniff out a stray treat that accidentally rolled between the cushions of the couch or detect any piece of food that inadvertently falls to the floor. That is how he discovered that dill pickles smell interesting but are not tasty. There is something magical about dogs and smells. They just seem to take time to enjoy the art of the smell.

The doorbell rang one day, and an older, oversized woman stood before me at the front door. She said she came to our home to introduce herself, but this slightly eccentric neighbor from diagonally across the street had met me many times while the kids played in the front yard. I invited her in and was taken aback by her immediate comment. "Your home smells like love." Rarely at a loss for words, I found myself perplexed by the statement. I remember laughing off her statement, thinking it must have been the vanilla-scented Glade Plug-Ins placed in most of the open wall sockets throughout the house or the scent of the lavender Fabuloso I used to mop the floors. After she left, I asked myself, "Can a home smell like love? If so, how?"

Smells are intriguing. When Michael was five, he had the most wonderful kindergarten teacher, Mrs. Hill. She had a soft spot for Michael, as Michael did for her. Daily, Michael put on Old Spice aftershave that had been left behind for him by his Papa or some expensive cologne samples his Aunt Crystal had given him. His sister Kimmy and I would revel in the wonderful smell of our five-year-old man sitting in the back seat of the car while we drove him to school.

A few weeks into school came meet-the-teacher night. I remember sitting behind the small desk in the tiny chair that was much too small for my over-sized behind. The entire experience made me feel rather like Goldilocks. Mrs. Hill addressed the class and then came around to personally introduce herself to each of the kinder parents. As she approached me, she stopped, smiled broadly, closed her eyes, and breathed in. "You must be Michael's mother. You smell as good as your son does." In that moment, we made a connection—a scent connection. For the rest of her life, Mrs. Hill became part of the fabric of who we were. To this day, even if I am only going to work out, take Sam for a walk, or just stop by Walmart, I wear perfume. Each scent reminds me of a place, a person, a time, an event, or a piece of clothing. I still have a bottle of perfume that, when I wear it, reminds me of our beloved Mrs. Hill.

As a manager, when I opened the door to my office each morning, it smelled like bubblegum or chocolate, both of which filled the jars on the credenza and were placed in easy reach for all passersby. My office was intentionally meant to be inviting, non-threatening. I always desired my scented office space to be a shared space. To me, it needed to smell of creativity, fun, and happy, not stacks of Xeroxed legal-sized papers. My car was the same way. The outside may have been smudged with the grimy residue of salt and dirty melted snow, but inside, it smelled like the bar of Zest soap tucked out of sight underneath the front seat.

Life and its moments have specific smells. There are Mountain Laurel trees in our current neighborhood that smell like grape Kool Aid. Our Schnoodle Fay used to love to stop and smell them. Then again, Fay stopped to smell everything! The smell of popcorn reminds me of my third-grade teacher who use to pop it in an electric popcorn popper for the entire class every time it rained in Phoenix (which was not very often.) She called it her rainy day special. The same smell of popcorn today can wake Schnoodle Sam up from a sound sleep. He eagerly waits for that one late popping kernel to suddenly pop out and escape from the pan and then drop to the floor for easy consumption.

The smell of Dawn dishwashing liquid and peroxide forever will remind me of skunk and the lesson learned—that the speed in which a gray Schnoodle named Fay can race through her doggie door after meeting said skunk in the back-yard on a cold rainy day, greatly exceeds the speed at which a 40-something-year-old woman can race to close off the doggie door before the skunk dog enters and rubs skunk smell all over the living room furniture. Poor Fay. She needed at least five Dawn dishwashing liquid, baking soda, and peroxide combination baths to oxidize the smell on her beard and face. We no longer own the couch.

And the musty smell of the first drops of rain hitting the blacktop pavement remind me that all things are mortal. For the rain brought about too many runaway Fay dog chases that could have ended badly. The rain brought about too many funerals for close friends and relatives that always ended sadly. Greta's and Fay's last goodbyes both took place in the rain.

There is one smell that still needs to be explored. It is the sweet smell of success. Like the smell of love, the smell of success is real. It is that sweet, wonderful, euphoric smell that fills our minds when we win the game. It is the happy smell that fills our hearts at a wedding, a graduation, or an awards celebration. It is the strong smell that fills a room after a great presentation or getting an A on a quiz. Or it's the smell of a job offer after a knock-it-out-of-the-ballpark interview. The sweet smell of success is why my offices were purposely designed to smell like bubblegum and chocolate and my homes like vanilla Glade Plug-Ins and lavender Fabuloso cleaner.

The sweet smell of success—it seems to come to people so rarely these days—needs to be enjoyed and celebrated. If you let it, the sweet smell of success can be imprinted on your very being, and it can trigger your mind to make all the painful, sad smells disappear.

As our car turns into our tiny subdivision, Schnoodle Sam quickly thrusts his head back out of the partially opened window for one final indulgent smell. With his eyes closed, he breathes in deep and recognizes the familiar smells of his neighborhood. Sam most likely recognizes the blend of Lantana, Rosemary, and Mexican Heather that line the flower beds on our street. As we round the corner, the dust from the neighbor's lawn blower mixes in with the smell of freshly cut Saint Augustine grass. Sam's nose begins to run, and he licks it to clear off the wetness. Perhaps he is resetting Pandora's box of familiar fragrances, knowing that his ride is coming to an end. He is getting ready for one final breath.

As our car stops in our driveway, the fuchsia pink Crepe Myrtle flowers fall from the tree branches and softly hit the windshield. Sam tucks his head back into the car and impatiently waits for the car door to open. Then his feet hit the pavement, and Sam races into the garage. One small Crepe Myrtle blossom clings to the shaggy bloomer of fur on his back leg. I imagine Sam will discover it later on while he is lying on his couch in the living room, still enjoying the smell of flowers dancing in his mind.

I will always be enamored by the childhood story of Ferdinand the bull, who just loved to sit and smell the flowers. Sam is my *Furr-dinand*. He reminds me that we all need to savor the flowers and once in a while just stop and enjoy their sweet smell

A Final Note

In dog years, I would be well over 400 years old by now and most likely dead, but I am thankful that I continue to survive in this dog eat dog world.

I could not have survived this long had it not been for the unconditional love I have been so blessed with.

I have served one Master who, on the sixth day, brought forth all living creatures after their kind.

I have raised two children who continue to love me regardless of my shortcomings and know that my bark is much worse than my bite.

I am married to a man who tolerates my need to walk every day, my need to have lots of toys, my need to be stroked once in a while, and who always appreciates my constant desire to be fed at least twice a day.

I have two older sisters who allow me to continually leave my mark as their baby sister - the runt of our litter.

I have been owned by six dogs who all have allowed me to love them as my fur-children.

It is by faith, family, and fur that I continue to survive in this Dog Eat Dog World.

About the Author

For more than three decades, Sanda Coyle has inspired people, grown managers, and developed sales talent while working for ABC, CBS, NBC and FOX television stations in New York, Arizona, and Texas. As Senior Vice President of Strategic Marketing, Vice President of Business Development, Director of Media Sales, General Sales Manager, Regional Sales Manager, National Sales Manager and Local Sales Manager, Sanda has had the privileged to serve iheartMedia, Meredith Corporation, Graham Media (Post Newsweek), United Chris Craft, New City (COX) Communications and others.

Sanda, together with her husband Robin Whitson, operate Coyle Whitson Strategy LLC. Sanda is an accomplished and energetic public speaker, consummate volunteer, and passionate dog lover.